Opening up
1 Samuel

JIM NEWHEISER

DayOne

One of my first (and most challenging) teaching assignments required me to explain 1 Samuel to a class of ten-year-olds over two semesters. The experience gave me a special love for that part of the Old Testament, and I never tire of revisiting it. Jim Newheiser's brief commentary is one of the richest, most insightful resources on 1 Samuel I have ever found. It is a well-written, compelling analysis of the biblical narrative, filled with razor-sharp reflections on the text, all very skillfully shown to be practical and applicable for today's readers. This is Old Testament exposition at its very best.

Phil Johnson, Executive Director, Grace to You, USA

1 Samuel is one of the most dynamic books of the Bible, a real page-turner, delightful for family devotions and for introducing congregations to the historical narratives of the Old Testament. Start here with Hannah, Samuel, the declension of Israel, the rise of Saul, the anointing of David, his friendship with

Jonathan, Goliath, the death of Samuel and the death of Saul. It is mouth-watering to savor those names and all they mean to the history of God's people. My friend Jim Newheiser, pastor and preacher, has opened up this narrative and shown us the lineage of the Messiah in the line of King David, and the powers of darkness that would have destroyed it. There is no better brief and helpful introduction to the first book of Samuel than the book you are holding in your hand right now. Devour it, and put its lessons into practice in your life and in the life of your church.

Revd. Geoff Thomas, Pastor since 1965 of Alfred Place Baptist Church, Aberystwyth, Wales

David is Christ; his followers are professing Christians; his foes are the enemies of Christ and his cause. Jim Newheiser's pointed study of the text of 1 Samuel shows how that book is truly part of Christian Scripture and that, at a time when Christ's right to rule the church and the world is challenged, all Christians are to be wholly on the Lord's side.

Hywel R. Jones, Professor of Practical Theology, Westminster Seminary, California, USA

I have listened to Jim Newheiser preach and teach God's Word for almost twenty years and consider him one of the finest expositors of our generation. He has now taken his expertise in the pulpit and has translated it into book form. *Opening Up 1 Samuel* is a helpful guide for interpreting 1 Samuel in a way that is exegetically faithful, highly practical, and thoroughly Christ-centered. This book is an incredible asset for anyone wanting to know and apply God's Word.

Benjamin L. Merkle, Professor of New Testament and Greek, Southeastern Baptist Theological Seminary, USA

Don't be fooled by the size of this volume into thinking that this one of those frustrating books that do little more than repeat the text. Jim Newheiser is a master at faithfully expounding the text and helpfully applying it. His commentary is rich in both insight and application. His faithful handling of the text means that this Old Testament historical book is shown to be full of contemporary relevance. The author points the reader to the person of Christ, not in some contrived and fanciful way, but with an

admirable integrity. I highly recommend this addition to the Opening Up series.

Colin D. Jones, Pastor, Three Bridges Free Church, UK

One of my first (and most challenging) teaching assignments required me to explain 1 Samuel to a class of ten-year-olds over two semesters. The experience gave me a special love for that part of the Old Testament, and I never tire of revisiting it. Jim Newheiser's brief commentary is one of the richest, most insightful resources on 1 Samuel I have ever found. It is a well-written, compelling analysis of the biblical narrative, filled with razor-sharp reflections on the text, all very skillfully shown to be practical and applicable for today's readers. This is Old Testament exposition at its very best.

Phil Johnson, Executive Director, Grace to You, USA

First printed 2011

ISBN 978-1-84625-326-3

British Library Cataloguing in Publication Data available
Published by Day One Publications
Ryelands Road, Leominster, England, HR6 8NZ
Telephone 01568 613 740 FAX 01568 611 473
email—sales@dayone.co.uk
web site—www.dayone.co.uk
North American e-mail—usasales@dayone.co.uk
North American website—www.dayonebookstore.com

Printed in the United States of America

With gratitude to the members of Grace Bible Church,
who patiently bear with my preaching and my absences,
and to my fellow church officers,
who so positively exemplify the qualities God seeks in those who would lead his people.

List of Bible abbreviations

THE OLD TESTAMENT

Gen.	Genesis
Exod.	Exodus
Lev.	Leviticus
Num.	Numbers
Deut.	Deuteronomy
Josh.	Joshua
Judg.	Judges
Ruth	Ruth
1 Sam.	1 Samuel
2 Sam.	2 Samuel
1 Kings	1 Kings
2 Kings	2 Kings
1 Chr.	1 Chronicles
2 Chr.	2 Chronicles
Ezra	Ezra
Neh.	Nehemiah
Esth.	Esther
Job	Job
Ps.	Psalms
Prov.	Proverbs
Eccles.	Ecclesiastes
S. of S.	Song of Solomon
Isa.	Isaiah
Jer.	Jeremiah
Lam.	Lamentations
Ezek.	Ezekiel
Dan.	Daniel
Hosea	Hosea
Joel	Joel
Amos	Amos
Obad.	Obadiah
Jonah	Jonah
Micah	Micah
Nahum	Nahum
Hab.	Habakkuk
Zeph.	Zephaniah
Hag.	Haggai
Zech.	Zechariah
Mal.	Malachi

THE NEW TESTAMENT

Matt.	Matthew
Mark	Mark
Luke	Luke
John	John
Acts	Acts
Rom.	Romans
1 Cor.	1 Corinthians
2 Cor.	2 Corinthians
Gal.	Galatians
Eph.	Ephesians
Phil.	Philippians
Col.	Colossians
1 Thes.	1 Thessalonians
2 Thes.	2 Thessalonians
1 Tim.	1 Timothy
2 Tim.	2 Timothy
Titus	Titus
Philem.	Philemon
Heb.	Hebrews
James	James
1 Peter	1 Peter
2 Peter	2 Peter
1 John	1 John
2 John	2 John
3 John	3 John
Jude	Jude
Rev.	Revelation

Contents

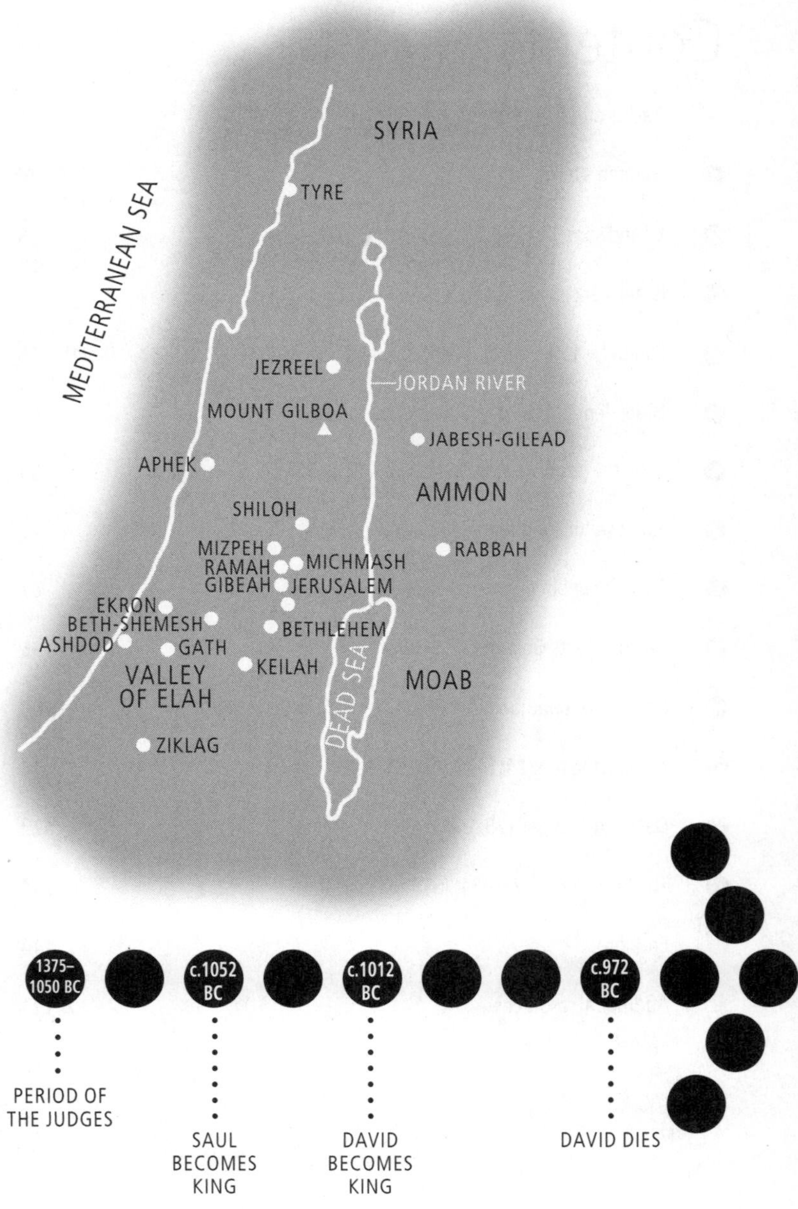
SYRIA
MEDITERRANEAN SEA
TYRE
JEZREEL
JORDAN RIVER
MOUNT GILBOA
JABESH-GILEAD
APHEK
AMMON
SHILOH
MIZPEH
RAMAH
MICHMASH
RABBAH
GIBEAH
JERUSALEM
EKRON
BETH-SHEMESH
BETHLEHEM
ASHDOD
GATH
KEILAH
VALLEY OF ELAH
DEAD SEA
MOAB
ZIKLAG
1375–1050 BC
c.1052 BC
c.1012 BC
c.972 BC
PERIOD OF THE JUDGES
SAUL BECOMES KING
DAVID BECOMES KING
DAVID DIES

Background and summary

We are facing a leadership crisis. We seek national leaders who will wisely guide us through times of economic turmoil and protect us from foreign enemies and domestic terrorists. Candidates often campaign as messiahs, offering hope and deliverance. Once they are elected, however, we are typically disappointed as they prove to be as ineffective and corrupt as those they replaced. Our churches also need strong leaders who will stand up for God's truth in an age of pluralism, compromise, and postmodern uncertainty. Sadly, many church leaders are as great a disappointment as our political leaders, because their lives don't live up to what they proclaim. They are more concerned about marketing the church to make it grow than about feeding and shepherding Christ's sheep. We also need leadership in our homes. Children need parents who will faithfully guide them in God's Word. Wives need husbands who will emulate the sacrificial loving leadership of Jesus. Many men have abdicated from this role and, as a result, their families suffer.

The book of 1 Samuel is the story of Israel seeking a leader. The Lord had chosen Abraham from among the nations of the earth and had given him great covenant promises of a land, a nation, and blessing. Centuries later, the Lord had multiplied Abraham's offspring and through Moses had led them out of Egypt. Then God, through Joshua, enabled his people to defeat the Canaanites and to occupy the land he had promised to Abraham. After Joshua's death came the troubled days of the judges in which a sad pattern emerged: the people would turn from God to sin and idolatry; the Lord would then bring judgment upon them through their enemies, the Canaanites, whom they had failed to drive completely from the land; the people in their misery would cry out to God; and the Lord would raise up a deliverer (a judge) to rescue them. After a season of peace the people would again turn from God and the pattern would repeat itself. The days of the judges were very dark days. The judges themselves, including Gideon and Samson, fell very short as leaders. The book of Judges ends with horrible scenes of civil war and massacre. The last verse summarizes the awful situation: "In those days there was no king in Israel; everyone did what was right in his own eyes" (Judg. 21:25).

The book of 1 Samuel begins in the dark days of the judges and records the transition to Israel's new system of government in which they are ruled by kings. The theme of 1 Samuel is Israel's need for a worthy leader. The book begins with Eli the priest judging Israel, but because Eli fails to restrain his wicked sons, Eli is deemed to be unworthy of having a dynasty to lead Israel (chs. 1–4). Samuel follows Eli as judge over Israel. He seeks to lead the nation in righteousness, but because his sons are also wicked, his family is also unfit to lead Israel (chs. 5–7). In Samuel's later years the Israelites demand a change in government. They want a king so that they can be like the other nations, in effect rejecting God as their King. The Lord gives them Saul, the people's king (chs. 8–12). After a promising start, Saul turns from the Lord and his ways (chs. 13–15); therefore, the Lord determines to install his king, the man after his own heart, in the place of Saul, the people's king. David, the son of Jesse, is chosen by God and proves himself worthy (chs. 16–18). King Saul, however, becomes jealous and seeks to murder David. The last chapters of 1 Samuel describe Saul's pursuit of David, which further displays Saul's wickedness and David's worthiness (chs. 19–30). The book ends with the tragic death of Saul (ch. 31), which then opens the way for the Lord's anointed one to reign as king over Israel (2 Sam.). While David proves to be a better king than Saul, even he falls short of God's standard (2 Sam. 11). Mere human leaders will fail. We need a better king, a divine king! Jesus Christ is the true and worthy King of God's people, of whom David is but a type.

How to read and understand 1 Samuel

While we are not certain who wrote 1 Samuel, we know that it can't have been Samuel because most of the book records events which took place after his death. Nor can we be sure when the book was written. Many believe it was written after the division of the kingdom of Israel, because there are references to Israel and Judah (11:8; 17:52; 18:16). We are certain, however, that this book infallibly records the history of Israel: "All Scripture is inspired by God ..." (2 Tim. 3:16a). We also know that 1 Samuel is not merely a collection of stories about people who lived a long time ago in a faraway place. This biblical book contains truth which is beneficial for us today: "... and [is] profitable for teaching, for reproof, for correction, for training in righteousness; so that the man of God may be adequate, equipped for every good work" (2 Tim. 3:16b–17). If we belong to the people of God, 1 Samuel is our story.

In this short commentary we will focus upon two particular ways in which 1 Samuel can benefit us. First, the events recorded in 1 Samuel are designed by God to teach us how to live today. Paul, writing about the historical events of the Old Testament, says, "Now these things happened to them as an example, and they were written for our instruction, upon whom the ends of the ages have come" (1 Cor. 10:11). Jesus makes moral application from an Old Testament event when he says, "Remember Lot's wife" (Luke 17:32). While biblical narratives typically record historical events without much comment or moral evaluation, these books are to be read through the lens of the teaching of the other sections of Scripture. These Old Testament stories powerfully illustrate the principles contained in God's law and in the wisdom literature. For example, Proverbs warns us that we ought to faithfully discipline our children and that the father who fails to chastise them will come to shame (Prov. 22:15; 29:15; 17:25), and the tragic story of Eli and his sons paints a full-color picture of this truth (1 Sam. 2–4). The law warns against the potential abuses of those who assume leadership (Deut. 17:14–20), and Saul's proud, despotic rule is a vivid warning to leaders and their hopeful followers of how power can be abused by frail, sinful men (and women). As we work our way through 1 Samuel we will take note of the practical life lessons God has for us and we will be reproved, corrected, trained, and equipped for good works.

Second, everything recorded in Scripture points to God's great work of redeeming his people through our Lord Jesus

Christ, of whom it was said after his resurrection, "Then beginning with Moses and with all the prophets, He explained to them [his followers] the things concerning Himself in all the Scriptures" (Luke 24:27). He said to them, "These are My words which I spoke to you while I was still with you, that all things which are written about Me in the Law of Moses and the Prophets and the Psalms must be fulfilled" (Luke 24:44). The history recorded in the Scriptures is not merely a record of random events. Everything which took place was part of the unfolding of God's magnificent plan of redemption. While the stories of the Old Testament have moral applications, they are not merely moral. For example, David was not just a great man who slayed giant Philistines. He was a type of Jesus, the Anointed of God, who defeats the enemies of his people. Ungodly leaders like Saul make us yearn for Jesus, the true King. My objective is to show you Christ on every page of 1 Samuel. You may be amazed to find much greater spiritual depth than you have ever seen before in some of the most familiar stories in the Bible.

Finally, my hope is that, as you go through 1 Samuel, you will learn to read all of Scripture, especially the historical narratives, in such a way that you will be able to find these truths for your own edification.

1 Hannah's hope

(1:1–2:11)

Does God care? First Samuel begins with the story of a woman, Hannah, whose heart is very heavy. In a culture in which a woman's significance is measured by her ability to have children, she is barren. Furthermore, her husband has taken a second wife, who not only has provided him with children, but also taunts Hannah for her childlessness. Hannah, in her distress, cries out to the Lord. He hears her cry and delivers her by blessing her with a son.

Hannah's story is like that of the nation of Israel, which is living in barrenness and being oppressed by enemies. Yet God has determined to rescue his people from oppression and to bless them with a deliverer. Hannah's son, Samuel, does not merely deliver her; he becomes the prophet who will anoint Israel's great king and deliverer. Hannah's story is also our story, because we too can cry out to God in our distress and receive deliverance through Christ.

God brings deliverance to his distressed people (1:1–28; 2:11)

We are introduced to an ordinary yet extraordinary family in Israel. Elkanah faithfully leads his family on an annual pilgrimage to worship the Lord through sacrifice (1:1–4). Because the temple has not yet been built in Jerusalem (v. 9 uses the word "temple" to refer to the meeting place in Shiloh, but the true temple of God was not built until generations later, under Solomon—1 Kings 6, 8), the place of worship is at Shiloh, where Eli and his sons serve as priests. This joyous occasion is marred, however, by the grief of one of Elkanah's two wives, Hannah, who is childless. Her misery is compounded by the cruelty of her rival wife. Elkanah, who dearly loves Hannah, is unable to comfort her (vv. 5–8). It is significant that our author reminds us that it is the Lord who has, to this point, closed Hannah's womb (v. 5b).

One might wonder how a good man like Elkanah could be a polygamist. While monogamy was God's design from the beginning (Gen. 2:18–25; Matt. 19:5, 8), he tolerated polygamy under the Old Covenant. It should be noted that polygamy always causes problems (Gen. 16; 30), as evidenced here by the rivalry of Elkanah's wives (1 Sam. 1:6–7).

Hannah, in her distress, cries out to God for a son and vows to dedicate him to the Lord (vv. 9–11). Eli the priest, seeing Hannah's mouth moving as she prays, wrongly assumes that she is drunk, and rebukes her (vv. 12–15). When Hannah explains what she was doing, Eli blesses her by praying that God will grant her petition (vv. 16–18).

After Hannah returns home with her family, the Lord remembers her and gives her the son for whom she yearns

(vv. 19–20). After Samuel is weaned she fulfills her vow and dedicates him to the Lord, taking him to Shiloh to serve with Eli in the house of the Lord (vv. 21–28; 2:11). Hannah's story ends happily as she sees Samuel every year when her family goes to Shiloh for sacrifice, and the Lord blesses her with more children (see 2:18–21).

Hannah sings praise to the Lord (2:1–10)

Hannah responds to God's goodness to her by composing a magnificent song of thanksgiving. She particularly praises God for powerfully delivering his helpless people from their enemies. He sovereignly reverses the plight of the oppressed as he brings down the wicked.

Hannah's song is strategically placed at the beginning of 1 Samuel because its significance goes far beyond her personal situation of barrenness and taunting from her rival wife. Hannah's song introduces the great themes of 1 and 2 Samuel and foreshadows the events which are to unfold. Hannah's barrenness and misery are a picture of the situation of God's people, Israel, who are weak and oppressed by their enemies among the Canaanites. Hannah, under the inspiration of the Holy Spirit, doesn't merely sing about her own situation; she sings prophetically for all God's people, who will soon be lifted up. Just as God provided a son to deliver Hannah, so he will provide a leader to rescue Israel from her enemies. Hannah concludes her song with a reference to Israel's king (given that the institution of the office of king is generations away, Hannah's song is prophetic) and anointed one (2:10), which is clearly a prophetic reference to David (16:13), who will deliver Israel from her enemies and bring stability and security to God's people. The counterpart to Hannah's song is found in David's songs of praise at the end of 2 Samuel (2 Sam. 22:1–23:7; originally 1 and 2 Samuel were one book, which would make the songs of Hannah and David bookends for the entire narrative). David, who wrote and sang generations after Hannah, uses much of the same vocabulary (e.g. words like horn, rock, salvation, darkness, thunder, anointed, and king) and develops similar themes as he reflects upon God's faithfulness in doing for Israel the things about which Hannah had sung many years before.

Where do we see Jesus in this passage?

The early chapters of 1 Samuel aren't primarily about Hannah; rather they are about the Lord, whose care for Hannah reflects his care for his people.

The deliverance of Hannah and Israel points to God's deliverance of his people through Christ. Just as Hannah was distressed because of her barrenness, so humanity is in great distress because of sin's devastating effects. Just as Hannah was oppressed by her rival, so we are oppressed by the world and the devil. Just as God provided a deliverer for Hannah and later for Israel, so God has sent his own Son, Jesus Christ, to deliver us from our spiritual barrenness and oppression. Through his work on the cross, Jesus has defeated Satan and set us free from sin. As a result, we enjoy the rich blessings of spiritual fruitfulness. First Samuel records events that were a significant part of the process by which God brought redemption to his people, as the office of king (which is one of the offices of Christ) was established, and David was anointed as the true king of Israel, of whom Jesus is the ultimate fulfillment.

The birth of Samuel, like the other miraculous births in the Bible (Gen. 21; Rom. 4:19–21), reminds us of Jesus's miraculous virgin birth (Isa. 7:14; 9:6–7). Samuel's birth also reminds us of the birth of John the Baptist, who, like Samuel, was a forerunner who acknowledged God's chosen king (Luke 1:5–25, 57–66).

Hannah's song looked beyond her personal deliverance to the deliverance of Israel by David and to the ultimate deliverance brought by God's anointed king, Jesus (1 Sam. 2:10; this is among the earliest uses of the Hebrew word for "anointed" in referring to the Messiah). Mary's song, known as the Magnificat, in which she sang of the deliverance to be brought through her son Jesus (Luke 1:46–55), shares many themes with Hannah's song. Like Hannah, Mary exalted the Lord and proclaimed how faithful he was to his covenant as he delivered his oppressed people, bringing down the proud and exalting the humble.

How does this passage apply to us?

There are many practical lessons to be learned from Hannah's story.

- God still uses ordinary people to accomplish his extraordinary purposes. Hannah, an ordinary wife in Israel, was chosen by God to bear Samuel, a man through whom God's plan of redemption would be advanced. Charles Spurgeon, whose ministry has influenced millions, was converted through the faltering efforts of a lay preacher.

Faithful mothers, Sunday school teachers, and friends may play a significant role in advancing God's purposes.

God still uses ordinary people to accomplish his extraordinary purposes.

- We see some biblical principles for the family exemplified. Just as the family of Elkanah, in their faithful worship, was a bright light in the dark days of the judges (1:3, 21), so we can be lights in a dark world as we honor God in our homes. Just as Hannah longed for children, so we also regard children as a blessing from God (Ps. 127) in a day in which children are sometimes seen as a nuisance and are killed in the womb. Just as Elkanah showed love to his wife Hannah and respected her judgment, saying to her, "Do what seems best to you" (1:23), so Christian husbands should show love and respect to their wives (Prov. 31:11a; 1 Peter 3:7). We also see, in the bitter rivalry between Elkanah's two wives, the consequences of violating God's design for marriage (one man with one woman for life, Gen. 2:24; Matt. 19:5).
- We need to be careful not to judge others according to appearances. When Eli saw Hannah's lips moving, he wrongly assumed that she was inebriated (1:12–16). Another example of misunderstanding based upon appearances happened at Pentecost, when some thought that the believers who were speaking in tongues were drunk (Acts 2:13–15). You might see a married woman out at a restaurant with a man you don't recognize and be tempted to assume that she is involved in an inappropriate relationship; but this man may simply be a cousin or

other family member. A preacher may see a man in the congregation with his eyes closed and think that he is not paying attention; but perhaps that man is meditating upon the sermon or praying in response to it. "Love ... hopes all things" (1 Cor. 13:4, 7): love assumes the best about others. Be careful to hear all the facts before drawing conclusions (Prov. 18:15, 17).

- God cares about our troubles and afflictions. Though Hannah was miserable, the Lord had a wonderful plan to do good through her trial, which ultimately came from him (1:5b). When we feel overwhelmed we must remember that God is aware of our situation and that he has not forsaken us (Heb. 13:5). Furthermore, we can trust that he has a good purpose in our trials (James 1:2–4; Rom. 8:28–39). We also receive comfort knowing that Christ was afflicted and is therefore able to sympathize with us in our weaknesses (Heb. 4:15).
- Hannah teaches us how to pray. She reverently called upon the Lord in her affliction (1:11). Sometimes God uses our tribulations to make us seek him more earnestly. When we are overwhelmed by trouble we should cry out to God with the expectation that he will hear us and give us peace (Phil. 4:6–7; 1 Peter 5:6). When God provided deliverance, Hannah praised God for his glorious attributes and for his works of deliverance for his people (2:1–10). The Lord answered Hannah's prayers in a way beyond that which she could have asked or imagined (Eph. 3:20). Like Hannah, we owe God thanksgiving and praise for his faithfulness to us in Christ.
- Our day is like the days of the judges (Judg. 21:25). We

live among people who are libertine and godless. Our nations and our churches are spiritually barren and lack leadership. The good news is that God has given a miraculous and gracious gift to his people through a son born to an ordinary woman. Just as Hannah cried out to the Lord "remember me" (1:11), so all of us who cry to God "remember me"—like the criminal who was crucified next to Jesus (Luke 23:42)—will experience God's great deliverance.

For further study ▶

FOR FURTHER STUDY

1. Why did God allow polygamy in Old Testament times?
2. Is there any difference between how women felt about having children in biblical times and how women should feel about having children today?
3. Should we formally dedicate our children to the Lord (Luke 2:23)?
4. Write down the similarities between Hannah's song (2:1–10), David's psalms (2 Sam. 22–23), and Mary's song of praise (Luke 1:46–55).
5. Liberation theologians, such as Jeremiah Wright, have used Hannah's song (2:1–10) to promote a Marxist view of social justice, siding with the oppressed against the rich and powerful. Can such an approach to this passage be justified?

TO THINK ABOUT AND DISCUSS

1. Why does God allow distress and persecution in the life of a believer?
2. Have you ever been misjudged based upon appearances? How have you misjudged others?
3. How can God use ordinary people for his extraordinary purposes today?
4. How can our families be lights in a dark world?
5. How is Hannah's dedication of Samuel to God unique? Is there any way in which we can emulate her as we think of our own children?
6. Use Hannah's song as a model from which you compose a personal prayer of thanksgiving and praise to God.
7. In what ways does this passage point to God's plan of redemption in Christ?

2 Eli and sons

(2:12–3:21)

All parents long to see their children turn out well. We especially yearn to see them walking with the Lord: "The father of the righteous will greatly rejoice, and he who sires a wise son will be glad in him" (Prov. 23:24). On the other hand, "A foolish son is a grief to his father and bitterness to her who bore him" (Prov. 17:25).

Eli is a God-fearing man who seeks to lead Israel wisely. At first glance he seems to be blessed because his sons are working with him, serving in the house of the Lord. But as we look into our text, we quickly see that Eli's sons are not like their father, but instead are corrupting the worship of the Lord. Eli becomes the classic case of parental failure as he fails to rein in his evil sons. Our text, however, is not merely about parenting. The big picture is that God is working through the downfall of Eli's family to bring new leadership to his people. In the short term, Samuel will replace Eli. In the mid-term, Samuel will anoint David to lead Israel as king. Ultimately, Jesus will be the King of his people.

Something is rotten in Shiloh (2:12–17, 22)

Eli's sons, Hophni and Phinehas, are described as "worthless men," literally "sons of Belial," who "did not know the LORD" (v. 12). What could be more tragic for the people of God than for those who are appointed to spiritual leadership being wicked men who do not fear the Lord? What occurred in Israel thousands of years ago (also see Ezek. 34:1–10) has continued throughout the history of the church, with corrupt clergy who have used their positions for selfish gain and have failed to shepherd God's people.

Eli's sons are guilty of several spiritual abuses. First, they are failing to obey the regulation of God's law for worship and sacrifice (vv. 13–14). The law made provision for the priests to be given a certain portion of the sacrifices (Lev. 7:31–34), but Eli's sons take whatever part of the meat they want. They also violate God's law by taking the meat before it has been burned and then strong-arming pious worshipers who seek to follow the Scriptures (vv. 15–16). In addition, they are guilty of sexual immorality with the women who serve with them in the tent of meeting (v. 22). In this, they are not only guilty of gross spiritual abuse, but they are also making the house of the Lord like the pagan temples, which often incorporated sex acts into their worship (Num. 25:1–3). In their abuse of their power and office Eli's sons resemble the arrogant about whom Hannah sang (v. 3). The greatest sin of the sons of Eli is their disregard of the Lord himself

(v. 17). Such worthless men will be brought down under the judgment of the Lord (vv. 4, 10, 25b).

The passive parent (2:22–29)

Eli is fully aware of the evil his sons are committing (vv. 22, 24). Eli, to his credit, does verbally admonish his sons as he seeks to put the fear of God into them (vv. 23, 25a). Hophni and Phinehas, however, pay no attention to their father's warning and continue in their sin (v. 25b). It is at this point that Eli fails. Because the tent of meeting and the priestly functions are under his authority, he is responsible for overseeing the work of his sons. Verbal warning is not enough. His rebuke should be backed up with action (3:13). At the very least, he could remove them from serving in the house of God. It may be that he should have had them executed as incorrigible sons (Deut. 21:18–21; if ever there was a case that fitted the scenario described in Deuteronomy, this is it).

Why does Eli fail to act? The reason is given by the man of God sent by the Lord to rebuke Eli (vv. 27–20): "Why do you kick at My sacrifice and at My offering which I have commanded in My dwelling, and honor your sons above Me, by making yourselves fat with the choicest of every offering of My people Israel?" (v. 29). Eli is guilty of honoring his sons above the Lord. (Note that the Hebrew word translated "honor" literally means "heavy." Eli treated his sons as "heavier" [more important] than the Lord. In verse 30, in a play on words, the Lord declares that, because Eli's house has failed to treat him as heavy, they will be lightly esteemed.) In other words, when push comes to shove, Eli chooses to please his sons at the expense of pleasing God. He is more concerned

Eli is more concerned about keeping the peace with his wicked sons than keeping the peace with God.

about keeping the peace with his wicked sons than keeping the peace with God. Apparently, Eli's guilt is compounded by the fact that he is sharing in the sacrificial meat which his evil sons are illicitly obtaining (eating all that ill-gotten meat may have contributed to Eli's death—see 4:18).

Judgment is pronounced on the house of Eli (2:30–34; 3:10–18)

God determines that Eli's family is unfit to lead Israel. Because they refuse to "honor" the Lord, they will be lightly esteemed by the Lord (2:30). Judgment is declared twice. First the man of God says that Eli's house will be cut off forever and that it will come to a sudden end, involving the deaths of Hophni and Phinehas (2:30–34). The same judgment is then revealed to Eli through Samuel (3:10–14). In response, Eli passively submits to God's decree (3:15–18).

God's judgment on Eli's sons is carried out when they both die in battle and the ark of the covenant is taken by the Philistines (4:11). When Eli hears the news, he falls over and dies (4:12–18). Interestingly, the shock which leads to Eli's death is not the news of the demise of his sons, but that of the loss of the ark of the covenant (4:18). So it appears that in his death Eli finally honors the Lord above his sons.

The Lord raises up a faithful leader for his people (2:26, 35–36; 3:1–9, 19–21)

While the Lord is bringing an end to the leadership of Eli's house, he is preparing Hannah's son, Samuel, to lead the nation. The man of God who visits Eli prophesies that a "faithful priest" will be raised up to serve in Eli's place (2:35–36). Samuel, in contrast to Eli's sons, fears God and serves faithfully alongside Eli (2:26; 3:1a). The Lord directly reveals himself to Samuel (3:1–9). As Eli's house is fading from view, Samuel is receiving and proclaiming the Word of the Lord, and his reputation grows throughout Israel (3:19–21).

It is interesting that Eli, who failed so miserably in raising Hophni and Phinehas, enjoys such great success in training Samuel. The difference is God's sovereign grace. It is also ironic that Eli nurtures and grooms his successor. In contrast to Saul, who will try to kill his successor (David), Eli submits to God's plan.

Where do we see Jesus in this passage?

We can see Christ in our passage in several ways. Jesus is the perfect Leader of God's people. In contrast to the poor leadership of Eli and his sons, Jesus is the Leader who honors and obeys God and does not fear men (John 17:4; Matt. 22:16). Rather than using his office in a self-serving way, he is the King who serves his people (Mark 10:45; Phil. 2:5–8) and the Priest who leads them into true spiritual worship (John 4:24; 14:6).

Samuel also serves as a type of Christ. His growth into maturity mirrors that of Jesus. Compare the description of Samuel in 2:26 with that of Christ in Luke 2:52: "Jesus kept increasing in wisdom and stature, and in favor with God and men." While God's promise in 1 Samuel 2:35 ("I will raise up for Myself a faithful priest who will do according to what is in My heart and in My soul; and I will build him an enduring house, and he will walk before My anointed always") applies to Samuel in the short term, the ultimate fulfillment is Christ, who surpasses Samuel as the faithful High Priest who will serve forever (Heb. 2:17; 5:10; 9:11–14). This reference to Christ's priestly office goes along with the earlier allusion to his kingly office in Hannah's song (2:10).

How does this passage apply to us?

We need godly, spiritual leaders who honor God

- "Those who honor Me I will honor, and those who despise Me will be lightly esteemed" (2:30). Sadly, many spiritual leaders today, like Eli's sons (2:12–17), abuse their position and power for selfish ends (3 John 1:9–10). Every year we hear reports of clergy who are involved in sexual and financial scandals. In many cases, such men either remain in their positions or are quickly restored to office. Some pastors are domineering over their flocks (1 Peter 5:3), demanding loyalty to themselves rather than to God. Some exert their own authority against that of God (Matt. 15:3) as they deny the teaching of Scripture on issues such as miracles, creation, and even justification by faith alone. Some spiritual leaders, like Eli (2:29), are more concerned about pleasing man than honoring God. In their desire to keep their members happy and to attract more people to their churches, they fail to fearlessly proclaim the whole counsel of God (Acts 20:27). Instead of regulating their worship according to Scripture (Acts 2:42; John 4:24), they design their meetings to please their human audience, often neglecting the biblical elements of worship while adding extra-biblical entertainment. Such leaders, because of their fear of man, are like Eli and fail to practice biblical church discipline. Professing Christians often compound the problem by choosing churches in which they feel comfortable and which have programs which meet their felt needs, rather than seeking fellowships with faithful leaders, bold biblical preaching, and reverent worship.

- The New Testament sets a high standard for our spiritual leaders (1 Tim. 3:1–7). They must be mature holy men who know God, in contrast to Eli's sons (2:12). They must be sexually pure and above reproach, especially in financial matters. They must faithfully preach the Word, without worrying about what their hearers might think of them (2 Tim. 4:1–5). They are called to lead God's people in reverent God-centered worship (Heb. 12:28), and they must maintain the purity of Christ's church. The church must remove leaders who disqualify themselves (Acts 20:29–31; 1 Tim. 5:20). The example of Eli and his sons should serve as a warning that when the leaders of God's people fail to honor him, he will remove them and replace them with faithful men (Ezek. 34:10, 23). Christians in churches whose leaders are not being faithful should first try to rectify the situation. If that doesn't work, they should seek to join a flock with faithful shepherds.

We need leadership in our homes

- We must learn from Eli, who is the most famous biblical example of a failed parent. Eli's fundamental mistake was that he honored his children above God (2:29). Scripture calls us to honor God in the way we raise our children, by seeking to discipline and instruct them in the Lord (Eph. 6:4). We dishonor the Lord when we turn a blind eye to our children's sin and fail to chastise them. Many parents, like Eli, avoid the conflict which typically comes with correcting our children. It may be true that letting your child have his or her own way will, in the short term, enable you to enjoy a certain measure of peace in your home, but in the end, "a child who gets his own way brings shame to his mother" (Prov. 29:15b). We must have God-centered, not child-centered, homes.

We dishonor the Lord when we turn a blind eye to our children's sin and fail to chastise them ... We must have God-centered, not child-centered, homes.

- Another important factor to notice is that Eli did not ignore the sins of his sons: he verbally admonished them. His error, however, was that he failed to accompany his rebuke with action. God's Word teaches that our children need to experience painful consequences for their sin: "Foolishness is bound up in the heart of a child; the rod of discipline will remove it far from him" (Prov. 22:15). The reason such discipline is necessary is illustrated by the proverb "A whip is for the horse, a bridle for the donkey, and a rod for the back of fools" (Prov. 26:3). If a donkey is refusing to obey you, neither gentle pleadings nor loud rebukes will motivate it. What it understands is pain. In the same way, foolish children do not readily heed verbal wisdom. "Fools despise wisdom and instruction" (Prov.

1:7b). What motivates them to change is pain. Many parents spend hours trying to reason with their children. When reason is not heeded they resort to either pleading or yelling. All the foolish child hears is nagging, and, like the donkey, he or she remains unmoved. Only firm, loving parental discipline will motivate the child to comply. The parents, like Eli, are afraid to bring painful consequences upon their child (Prov. 29:25) and so contribute to the child's ruin. "Discipline your son while there is hope, and do not desire his death" (Prov. 19:18).[1]

- A remarkable feature about this passage is that Eli's famous failure occurs when his children are adults. As we continue to read, we will see that Samuel and David experienced similar failures with their adult children. What happened in Eli's household is being repeated in our day as parents continue to enable the sins of their adult children. While we cannot control or be held responsible for the actions of our children when they are independent, we are responsible for what they do while they are living under our roofs and receiving our support. Eli was responsible for the sins of his adult sons because they were working under his authority in the priestly service. Many parents in our day are providing their adult children with rooms, board, vehicles, insurance, cell phones, and money, in spite of the fact that their adult children are sexually immoral, lazy, financially irresponsible, and abusing substances. While such parents may nag and whine, they, like Eli, are afraid to take their support away or to kick their children out of the house, which makes them enablers who are bringing God's judgment upon their homes.[2]

- There is also a lesson for children in this passage. You are responsible for your choice between the Lord and sin, and you can't blame your parents for how you turn out. While Eli was far from a perfect parent and was held responsible for his failures (3:13), his sons were responsible for their sinful choices. They rejected the wise instruction of their father (2:25; Prov. 15:5). Samuel, on the other hand, was also raised by Eli, but he heeded Eli's teaching and was blessed (2:26; 3:1). "Hear, my son, your father's instruction and do not forsake your mother's teaching" (Prov. 1:8). If you dishonor your parents, as Hophni and Phinehas did, you will be under God's judgment (Prov. 30:17). On the other hand, you can be like Samuel, who honored Eli and God from an early age (2:26; 3:1).
- Because we are imperfect sinful parents and because our children are by nature foolish, we desperately need God's sovereign grace, which alone can save us and our children (John 6:44).

FOR FURTHER STUDY

1. What factors determine why children turn out the way they do? Why did Abel honor the Lord while Cain was a murderer (Gen. 4)? See Ezekiel 18:5–32 and Luke 2:51–52.
2. Eli's sons failed to follow the regulations for Old Covenant worship. What are the regulations for worship under the New Covenant? How are these being violated today?
3. What are the qualifications for our spiritual leaders? In light of the fact that none of us is perfect, how strictly should these be applied?
4. While Eli's submission to God's judgment seems pious, should he have done more (i.e. repent), in light of the Lord's stated willingness to relent from judgment? What could he have done? (See 3:18; Jer. 18:7–8; Jonah 3:1–10; 1 Kings 21:27–29.)
5. Our text says that the Lord was determined to put Hophni and Phinehas to death (2:25). How can this be reconciled to their responsibility for their sin? Also see Romans 9 (especially in the treatment of Pharaoh).
6. What was God doing in this section of Scripture to advance his plan for his people?
7. To whom does the promise of 1 Samuel 2:35 refer?

TO THINK ABOUT AND DISCUSS

1. What harm has come in our day from worthless men who do not know God serving in the house of the Lord (1 Sam. 2:12)?
2. The Old Covenant provided for the stoning of incorrigible children (Deut. 21:17–21). What should be done with incorrigible young adults in our day?
3. What should parents expect of their adult children who are living on their support? What should parents do if these expectations are not being met?
4. How can we see Jesus in this passage?

3 Israel's ark is raided and lost

(4:1–7:2)

In the movie *Raiders of the Lost Ark* Indiana Jones vies to find the ark of the covenant before the Nazis can get it because of the belief that any army who carries the ark into battle will be victorious over its enemies. Dr. Jones and his Nazi antagonists could have saved themselves a lot of time if they had read 1 Samuel 4–6.

In this passage the Israelites try to use the ark as a magic talisman in battle and are soundly defeated by the Philistines, who capture the ark and then encounter troubles of their own. In these events the Lord shows himself to be holy and sovereign. He cannot, unlike the false gods of the nations, be manipulated by men.

Israel loses two battles and the ark (4:1–22)

After the mention of Samuel at the beginning of this section (4:1), he is not mentioned during the rest of the account of Israel's defeats and the loss of the ark. This probably reflects the reality that the people are relying upon their own devices in the midst of their crises, rather than turning to God's prophet to receive guidance and help. Later, when they turn to Samuel to lead them, they receive deliverance (7:1–14).

While all Scripture is God-breathed, the chapter divisions are not divinely inspired. This is one of several places in Scripture where it appears that the beginning of one chapter relates more to the content at the end of the preceding chapter than to the chapter which follows.

The situation in Israel is dire. Their archenemies, the Philistines, with whom they are in competition for territory and power, have defeated them in a battle in which thousands have been killed (4:1–2), and further warfare lies ahead. The Philistines lived on the coastal plain bordering Israel. They were a seafaring people who were apparently eager to expand their territory. They also had more advanced weapons than the Israelites.

Whenever a nation loses a battle it is time for self-examination. The leaders of Israel are right to realize that their defeat is ultimately because of the Lord (v. 3a). God often used pagan nations like the Philistines to chastise his people for their sins and idolatry. Yet while Israel asks the right question—"Why has the LORD defeated us today?"—their solution is the wrong one. Rather than repenting of their sins (Deut. 28:15, 25) and seeking guidance from the Word of the Lord through the prophet Samuel, they decide to try to harness God's power by bringing the ark of the covenant into battle with them (vv. 3b–4). The ark of the covenant symbolized the presence of God among his people. It was a box four feet by two feet by two feet which contained the tablets of stone (the Ten Commandments), a jar of manna, and Aaron's rod which budded. On the lid, which was the mercy seat, were two golden angelic figures, reminding God's people of his holiness. It was the holiest place where, once a year, the high priest would make atonement for God's people.

The use of the ark as a magic talisman was not commanded in God's law and instead imitated the superstitions of the pagan nations, who believed that their gods were localized and could be manipulated. Rather than humbling themselves before God, Israel tried to use him, like a genie, for their purposes. The Lord refuses to allow himself to be put under anyone's power.

> The Lord refuses to allow himself to be put under anyone's power.

While the appearance of the ark on the battlefield initially gives confidence to the Hebrews and puts fear into the heart of their enemies (vv. 5–9), in the end Israel is defeated yet again. Even worse, this time the ark is captured and taken away by the Philistines (vv. 10–11). Furthermore, Eli and his sons all die. The glory has truly departed from Israel, as is symbolized when Eli's grandchild, born in the aftermath of the events in which his father, his uncle, and his grandfather died and the ark was captured, is named Ichabod, which means "no glory" (vv. 21–22).

The Lord can defend himself (5:1–12)

After the Philistines capture the ark of God they take it to one of their great cities as a trophy of war, perhaps hoping to harness its powers for their own purposes (vv. 1–2). This is similar to what the Philistines did when they captured Samson (Judg. 16:23–25). Another example from history is when the English defeated the Scots in 1296 and took the Stone of Scone, upon which the kings of Scotland had been crowned, and incorporated it into the coronation chair in London's Westminster Abbey (it has since been returned to Scotland).

The Philistines put the ark into the temple of their god, Dagon, symbolizing Dagon's conquest of the Lord who appeared to be unable to help his people when the Philistines defeated them on the battlefield. In the eyes of the Philistines the Lord, like his people, is under their power.

While the Philistines boastfully imagine that the Lord has fallen into their hands, in reality it is the other way around. And "it is a terrifying thing to fall into the hands of the living God" (Heb. 10:31). The Philistines are ripe for judgment. The morning after they place the ark of the Lord's presence in their pagan temple they find that their god, Dagon, has fallen down, symbolically bowing before the Lord. Because he is helpless, the Philistines have to set their idol upright again, only to find that the next day Dagon's head and hands are cut off. These events are a reminder of the scriptural texts mocking the idols of the nations and contrasting them with the Lord God:

Our God is in the heavens;
He does whatever He pleases.
Their idols are silver and gold,
The work of man's hands.
They have mouths, but they cannot speak;
They have eyes, but they cannot see;

They have ears, but they cannot hear;
They have noses, but they cannot smell;
They have hands, but they cannot feel;
They have feet, but they cannot walk;
They cannot make a sound with their throat.
Those who make them will become like them,
Everyone who trusts in them.

(Ps. 115:3–8; also see Isa. 44:9–20)

Dagon is helpless before the Lord, and the Philistines are about to become like their idol.

After this, the Lord smites the Philistines living in and near Ashdod with painful tumors (v. 6). When the people of Ashdod refuse to keep the ark any longer, they send it to the other leading Philistine cities of Gath and Ekron, where further havoc is wreaked (vv. 7–10). Finally, the Philistine leaders determine to send the ark of God back to Israel, with the hope that God's hand of judgment will be lifted (vv. 11–12). They are forced to realize that their conquest of Israel does not imply that they have defeated the Lord.

The ark is returned (6:1–7:2)

The Philistines are now more eager to get rid of the ark than they had been to capture it in the first place. Their holy men devise a way to return the ark to Israel by placing it, along with their guilt offerings, on an unmanned cart pulled by two cows (6:1–9). The Philistine leaders show an odd mixture of pagan superstition (6:3–5), the fear of God (6:6), and uncertainty (6:7–9). The Lord miraculously causes the cows to return to Israel (cows which had never been yoked would not naturally have walked in unison, away from their calves, to Israel); there the people receive the ark with gladness and offer sacrifices to the Lord (6:13–16). The glory has returned to Israel (4:22). The Lord has defeated Dagon, whose worshipers admit defeat and pay a ransom (6:17–19). The Lord liberates his ark so that his people can be liberated from their idolatry and unbelief.

The celebration is marred when the men of Beh-shemesh do not respect the holiness of God and look into the ark, resulting in many deaths. Due to a dispute over the Hebrew text and its translation, the number appears as seventy in some versions and 50,070 in others. Either way, the point is that it is deadly to trifle with the holy things of God. Later, Uzzah will be struck down under similar circumstances (2 Sam. 6:6–7).

After this, the ark is moved to Kiriath-jearim, where it remains for twenty years, during which time Israel continues to lament (7:2). Even though they have their ark back, their internal and external troubles remain.

Where do we see Jesus in this passage?

Jesus replaces the ark of the covenant as the place where men and women meet God. He has made the atonement for our sins in the Holy of Holies (Heb. 9:3–14), which the ark foreshadows. Through his blood we can safely draw near to God (Eph. 2:13), entering his holy presence. Jesus is the glory of God (John 1:14; 17:24) who will never depart (1 Sam. 4:22) from his people (Matt. 28:20).

Though we, like the Philistines, have gone astray and worshiped idols such as materialism and pleasure, God struck Jesus so that he will not have to strike us (Isa. 53:4–6).

The Philistines sensed the need for a guilt offering to the Lord (1 Sam. 6:17), but their offering did not actually atone for sin. Jesus's offering of himself has forever removed our guilt (Isa. 53:10; Heb. 10:14).

How does this passage apply to us?

- Just as the people of Israel suffered defeat because God was chastising them (4:3), so your suffering may be because God is chastising you (Ps. 32:3–4; Prov. 3:11–12).
- People still try to manipulate God, just as the Israelites did when they took the ark into battle (4:3). Some believe that they gain God's protection through certain objects, such as religious jewelry. Such practices resemble the superstitions of pagans who ascribe luck, power, and success to objects such as crystals or a rabbit's foot (Deut. 18:9–14). Others bargain with God, expecting that he will bless them for their outward religious acts, such as repeating prayers or crossing themselves. False religious teachers in the word-faith movement claim that we can harness God's power to give us wealth and healing as we learn how to speak to God with authority. But God is not a genie whom we can manipulate to fulfill our whims. Those who have tried have paid a significant price; for example, the sons of Sceva fled naked and wounded (Acts 19:14–17). God is sovereign and free. He does as he pleases (Isa. 46:8–11). The power of God in this age is manifested not through an ark or through buildings or relics, but in the gospel (Rom. 1:16–17; 1 Cor. 1:18–25; Heb. 4:12).
- People today, like the Philistines, worship idols (Rom. 1:25). Our idols don't outwardly resemble the stone

statue of Dagon, but they are just as dangerous, as we seek security in material things ("greed, which amounts to idolatry," Col. 3:5) or devote ourselves to earthly pleasures ("whose god is their appetite," Phil. 3:19). Like Dagon, our idols are unable to protect us or satisfy us (Isa. 55:1–2). Sooner or later they will topple. It is sad that, after seeing the Lord conquer their idol, the Philistines sent away the ark of the covenant and then went back to worshiping their worthless statue. Yet that is exactly what so many of us do. Though our idols continually let us down, we stubbornly continue pursuing them, propping up their failed idolatrous worldviews rather than turning to the Lord. May God help us to continually turn away from earthly idols and trust him alone (1 John 5:21).

- One of the religious idols of our age is pluralism, the idea that all religious viewpoints are equally valid. Such a viewpoint would look upon worship of Dagon and worship of the Lord as essentially the same. People today might say that the Israelites and the Philistines were worshiping the same deity, just by different names, and that neither could judge the other's religion. Scripture, however, teaches that there is only one God (Deut. 6:4) and that the only way to know him is through his Son, Jesus Christ (John 14:6). False religions are not to be admired or respected, but are under God's judgment (2 Cor. 10:5).

False religions are not to be admired or respected, but are under God's judgment.

- When the people of Beth-shemesh looked into the ark,

they perished, because they failed to respect the holiness of the Lord (6:19). We too must respect God's holiness. God's name is holy and is not to be used in vain (Exod. 20:7). Jesus is the Holy One of God. Those who refuse to honor him defy God and invite his judgment.

FOR FURTHER STUDY

1. Read Exodus 25:10–22 and try to picture in your mind's eye what the ark of the covenant must have looked like.
2. How did the ark portray the work of Christ? See Hebrews 9:1–14.
3. Would it matter if we were to find the ark of the covenant today? Why or why not?
4. If we were to find the ark, would it have any supernatural power? Explain your answer, using Scripture.

TO THINK ABOUT AND DISCUSS

1. Is there any sense in which the glory of God can depart from a place today (see Rev. 2–3)? Where is the glory of God manifested today?
2. What are some of the ways in which people try to manipulate God today? Have you ever been guilty of this?
3. What idols do people worship in our day?
4. How is religious pluralism manifested in our world today? How should we interact with people of other religions?
5. How does God chastise his people today? Does God chastise entire nations? Churches?
6. How can you know if your suffering is God's discipline?
7. How does this passage point to Christ?

4 Samuel leads Israel in repentance and revival

(7:1–17; 3:1–14, 19–21)

Repent! The preaching of repentance has fallen out of fashion in our day of seeker-sensitive mega-churches. Yet it is significant that both Jesus and John the Baptist began their public ministries proclaiming a message of repentance to Israel: “Repent, for the kingdom of heaven is at hand” (Matt. 3:2, 8; 4:17). The apostles were also sent forth to preach repentance (Acts 2:37–38), and Jesus calls wayward churches to repent (Rev. 2:5, 16, 22; 3:3, 19).

In the Old Testament the Lord frequently calls his people to repentance (Ezek. 14:6). In 1 Samuel 7 we find that Israel’s unfaithfulness has led to her oppression under the Philistines. However, when God’s people repent and finally turn from their sin to him, he is gracious in restoring and reviving them.

Israel is driven to repentance (7:1–2)

Israel's situation is desperate. After being defeated by the Philistines in battle, the Israelites tried to use the ark of the covenant as a kind of magic charm, only to be conquered yet again, this time losing the ark. Because the hand of the Lord was heavy on the Philistines, the ark was returned, but because the Israelites did not properly regard the Lord's holiness, many were struck dead (6:19).

The ark is then stored in Kiriath-jearim and for twenty long years Israel continues to endure oppression from the Philistines. Finally, following the pattern set in the days of the judges (Judg. 2:11–19; 3:9; 4:3), the people cry out to the Lord in lamentation, and the Lord delivers them.

A prophet is among them (3:1–14, 19–21)

Twenty years earlier the Lord raised up Samuel, the son of Hannah, as a prophet for Israel (3:1–14). A prophet was a person who infallibly spoke for God, to whose word the people had to submit (Deut. 18:18–22). Prophets were very rare in those days, probably because of the sinfulness of the people (3:1; Amos 8:11–12). God himself called Samuel at an early age (3:1–14). All Israel acknowledged that Samuel was a prophet through whom the Lord spoke powerfully (3:19–21). Yet it appears that for two decades the people of Israel showed no interest in hearing God's message through Samuel. They did not consult him before implementing their disastrous scheme of carrying the ark of the covenant into battle. Nor did they seek his counsel when the Philistines returned the ark, their mishandling of which led to further disaster. Now, after many more years have passed, their affliction has become unbearable and they are ready to listen to the man of God.

Repentance and revival (7:3–9)

Samuel proclaims to Israel a message of repentance. The word "repent" means "turn." Samuel calls God's people to turn from their foreign idols and serve the Lord alone (v. 3). He also promises that when they do this, the Lord will deliver them. The Israelites respond in faithful obedience by removing their Baals and determining to serve only the Lord (v. 4). The people go with Samuel to Mizpah to worship the Lord, confessing their sins with fasting (v. 6). They acknowledge Samuel's position as judge and leader of the people of God. The tension at Mizpah is heightened by the fact that the Philistines, seeing that Israel has gathered, are coming forth for battle (v. 7). The prophet intercedes and offers sacrifices on behalf of the people, and the Lord graciously hears his cries (vv. 5, 8–9). Revival has broken out!

Deliverance (7:10–17)

The Philistines come up against the Israelites, perhaps hoping to deal them a final, decisive blow. But this time, unlike in previous battles, the Philistines are soundly defeated (vv. 10–11). What makes the difference? It is not that the Israelites invent new weapons. Nor do they employ a clever new military strategy. The sole cause of their victory is that the Lord is with them. He who controls all things causes a great thunder which confuses the Philistines and he gives his people strength to win the battle. Israel's enemies are driven back and the nation enjoys a time of peace under Samuel's leadership (vv. 13–17). Samuel places a stone of remembrance, which he names Ebenezer, to commemorate the Lord's great victory, for the glory is all the Lord's (v. 12).

Where do we see Jesus in this passage?

Jesus is the final great Prophet of whom Samuel (3:20) and all the other prophets were only a shadow and a type (Deut. 18:15). Jesus, like Samuel (1 Sam. 7:3), came preaching repentance to Israel (Matt. 7:14). Jesus, like Samuel (1 Sam. 7:5, 8–9), intercedes for his needy people (Heb. 7:25; Rom. 8:34), and God hears his pleas for us. While Samuel sacrificed a lamb to atone for the sins of the people (7:9), Jesus is the true Lamb of God, who turns away God's wrath and brings salvation to his people (John 1:29). Just as Samuel led the people in defeating their enemies the Philistines (7:13), so Jesus has defeated our souls' enemies: sin, Satan, and death (Gen. 3:14; Rom. 16:20; Col. 2:15; 1 John 3:8). While Samuel brought a season of peace to Israel (7:14), Jesus brings everlasting peace to his people (Isa. 9:6; Eph. 2:14; Rom. 5:1). Those who refuse to listen to Jesus, God's great Prophet, are under God's judgment (Deut. 18:19).

How does this passage apply to us?

- Does God speak to people today as he spoke to Samuel? God's final great revelation of himself has been given in the person and work of Jesus: "God, after He spoke long ago to the fathers in the prophets in many portions and in many ways, in these last days has spoken to us in His Son" (Heb. 1:1–2a). The foundation for the church has been laid by the apostles and prophets who wrote the completed New Testament (Eph. 2:20). Therefore, while we do not expect more prophets giving new revelation, God does speak to us through his infallible Word (2 Tim. 3:16–17). God also speaks to us through our pastors and teachers, who faithfully proclaim and expound God's Word to us (2 Tim. 4:1–2). We know those whom God has called, not through an audible call like that of Samuel, but by recognizing those whom God has gifted and qualified (1 Tim. 3:1–7; Acts 20:28). We need bold preachers like Samuel, who will faithfully proclaim God's Word to us, even when we are wayward. Those false teachers and false prophets who go beyond Scripture with their extra-biblical traditions (Matt. 15:3, 9) or claims of further revelation mislead many and cause great harm to the church (2 Peter 2:1; Mark 13:22).

- We too need to repent of our sin. The people of Israel suffered many defeats and sorrows because they had wandered from God. Eventually, their afflictions drove them to turn from their sins to God, who then delivered them. God continues to call us to repentance, often using our troubles to drive us to himself (Ps. 119:67, 71). Repentance is the part of the gospel message that states that we need to turn from our sin to Christ (Acts 2:38; 17:30; Luke 13:3; 24:47). Sadly, many preachers today are reluctant to rebuke sin and plead with people to repent. Often their messages are man-centered offers of human happiness and enhanced self-esteem. But we cannot be saved unless we know and acknowledge our great need. Jesus said, "It is not those who are well who need a physician, but those who are sick. I have not come to call the righteous but sinners to repentance" (Luke 5:31–32). Spurgeon wrote, "If God means to save you, he will make you lament after him."[1] Those who humbly repent before God, like the Israelites, receive his saving deliverance (Luke 18:9–14). God's grace to the Israelites after twenty years of unfaithfulness and idolatry gives hope to all that God gladly welcomes sinners, in spite of their longstanding rebellion against him. Repentance is not a one-time event for a believer. Because we continue to sin after conversion, we must continue to humbly confess our sins to God, with the confidence that he will forgive us for Christ's sake (1 John 1:8–2:2). Just as the Israelites' repentance was expressed through the action of putting away their idols (1 Sam. 7:4), so our repentance should be expressed in action (2 Cor. 7:10–11) as we take drastic measures to destroy our idols (Matt. 5:29–30).

Repentance is not a one-time event for a believer.

- Do nations still repent today? The repentance of Israel was a national repentance which led to national blessing. Some seek to apply this Old Testament principle to nations today, using verses such as "If … My people who are called by My name humble themselves and pray and seek My face and turn from their wicked ways, then I will hear from heaven, will forgive their sin and will heal their land" (2 Chr. 7:13–14). While certainly our nations are guilty before God and worthy of his judgment, no nation today can claim to be the people of God, as Israel was under the Old Covenant. (There are biblical examples of a kind of repentance among pagan nations, including Nineveh in Jonah 3 and within Babylon in Daniel 4. These nations, however, never enjoyed status as God's people.) God's holy nation in this age is his church (1 Peter 2:9). Jesus calls churches to repent (Rev. 2:5, 16, 22) and warns that they will face consequences if they do not turn from their sins. Our churches stand in need of repentance for many things, including a lack of faithfulness to God's Word, worldliness (James 4:4), and a failure to evangelize. We, like Israel, should turn away from our idols to serve God alone.

- Should we expect to see revival like that which Israel experienced? Think of Samuel, who for twenty years declared the Word of God but was virtually ignored by the people. Then suddenly they came to him, eager to hear and to turn to the Lord. What happened? Did Samuel change his message to make it more acceptable to the people of his age? Did he start telling funny stories in his sermons? Did he change his worship style and music to appeal to the young people? Samuel kept faithfully proclaiming the Word, and God sovereignly determined that it was time to revive his people. Similar patterns have continued in the history of the church. A man who has been faithfully preaching the gospel message while seeing little fruit suddenly sees many of the lost converted and those who were already saved revived in their faith. Then, just as suddenly, the revival ends and things settle down into a more ordinary pattern of church life. What makes the difference? It is not human technique. It is God, choosing to move where and when he is pleased to glorify himself (John 3:8). Just as Samuel continually prayed for God's people (1 Sam. 12:23) and stood ready to give them God's Word, so we should employ the same means, hoping that God will add his blessing.

For further study ▶

FOR FURTHER STUDY

1. In what sense is Jesus the final Prophet (Heb. 1:1–2)?
2. Do we have prophets today (Eph. 2:20)?
3. What was the standard for someone who claimed to be a prophet? Could he or she ever be wrong (Deut. 18:15–22)?
4. To whom does the promise of revival after repentance in 2 Chronicles 7:14 apply? To nations? To churches? To individuals?
5. Is there ever a time when we should place an Ebenezer, to remember what God has done for us?

TO THINK ABOUT AND DISCUSS

1. If we don't have prophets among us, how does God speak to his people today?
2. What are the similarities and the differences between a preacher and a prophet?
3. Does God call people in our day in the same way in which he called Samuel (3:1–10)?
4. What should we do if we want to see revival in our day?
5. Where can we see Jesus in 1 Samuel 7?

5 Israel demands a king

(8:1–22; 12:1–25)

Every time there is a political election, people get excited, believing that this is their opportunity to elect a government that will bring prosperity, peace, and justice. Campaigns promise hope and change, and leaders pledge that they have the character and integrity to root out corruption and waste from government. Weeks or months after the election, when the new government proves to be no better than the old, the electorate becomes disillusioned.

In this passage the people of Israel decide that it is time for a change of government. They believe that a king is better able to give them security from their enemies than the judges who have been serving them for so long. The prophet Samuel is grieved and warns them that their desire dishonors God, whom they are rejecting as their King, and will have unpleasant consequences. When the people insist, they get the king they ask for and deserve.

Give us a king! (8:1–9)

Samuel has been faithfully judging Israel for many years. He has led the nation to victory over the Philistines and ushered in a time of peace. The elders of Israel are now concerned (vv. 1–5) because Samuel is getting old and will not be able to lead the nation much longer. His sons, whom he appointed to share the responsibility for judging the people, are not fit to replace him. They are, like the sons of Samuel's mentor, Eli, corrupt and abuse their power by taking bribes (Deut. 16:19). What the elders of Israel ask, however, is not merely for a new judge, but for an entirely new system of government. During the era of the judges, Israel functioned as a tribal confederation and the Lord ruled his people, raising up leaders as needed to face a crisis (Judg. 2:16, 18; 3:10, 15; 6:12; 11:29). Now the people demand a powerful hereditary king who will lead the nation against her enemies (v. 20).

Samuel is displeased by their request. This is not the first time the nation has sought a king. Many years earlier the people sought to make Gideon their king, but he refused (Judg. 8:22–23). What is wrong is not their desire for a king, for God said that one day Israel would be ruled by a king (Gen. 49:10; Deut. 17:14–20). What is wrong is their motive for seeking a king. The Israelites want to be "like the other nations" (vv. 20, 5). But Israel was chosen by God to be different from the surrounding nations: "Thus you are to be holy to Me, for I the LORD am holy; and I have set you apart from the peoples to be Mine" (Lev. 20:26). God is to be their King and their glory. When the time came for them to have a king, this king would be different from the kings of the nations because he would serve under the Lord's authority. Yet by the way the people of Israel are requesting a king, they are guilty of rejecting the Lord as their King (vv. 7–8). Whenever Israel has turned to the Lord, he has faithfully delivered them from their enemies (7:10). Now they are looking to an earthly monarch, rather than to the Lord for their security.

> Do not trust in princes,
> In mortal man, in whom there is no salvation.
> His spirit departs, he returns to the earth;
> In that very day his thoughts perish.
> How blessed is he whose help is the God of Jacob,
> Whose hope is in the LORD his God.
>
> (Ps. 146:3–5)

Whichever king they choose will one day die. Why would they want a dynasty or expect that their king's sons will turn out any better than the sons of Eli or Samuel? They should have waited for the Lord's timing to receive a king in his own way.

Though Samuel is grieved by the people's request, the Lord instructs him to give the people the king they desire (vv. 7, 9). Samuel is also charged to warn the people of what will happen when they get their king. God will give them exactly the king they deserve, which should make them long for God's King.

Your king will cost you (8:10–22)

Samuel speaks prophetically of what will happen to Israel under this new king (v. 10). Israel will become like the surrounding nations in all the worst ways. The sad fulfillment of Samuel's prediction is recorded in the rest of 1 and 2 Samuel, plus 1 and 2 Kings.

Samuel warns that as the king expands his power, he will draft Israel's sons into the military (vv. 11–12) and take their daughters to serve in his household (v. 13). He will tax the people heavily to pay for his programs (vv. 14–17a), while giving some of their property to his cronies (v. 14; 22:7; 1 Kings 21:7). The people's freedom will be taken away and they will be like slaves of the king (v. 17b). Finally, when they realize their folly (and that they were better off without a king) and cry out to God, God will make them live with their tragic choice (v. 18).

The people are not persuaded by Samuel's warnings and remain adamant that they must have a king so that they can be like the other nations (vv. 19–20). They believe that they know better than the Lord what is best for them, so God gives them the king for whom they ask (vv. 19–22).

Samuel's farewell (12:1–25)

A few chapters later, after Saul is established as king, Samuel gives a farewell address to the people he has led, again warning them of the consequences of demanding a king. He reminds them of his own integrity (vv. 3–5), which is in contrast to that of their coming king, and of the Lord's faithfulness to his covenant (vv. 6–11). All this implies that they had no good reason to seek a king (v. 12). Yet Samuel promises that God will bless them if they remain faithful to God's covenant. If they break his covenant, however, they will be cursed (vv. 13–18). Finally, he reassures the people of his ongoing prayers for them (vv. 19–25). Samuel, with his personal integrity, boldness in proclaiming the Word of God, and faithfulness in intercessory prayer, is a model for spiritual leaders.

Though Samuel is old, he is not done. He lives long enough to see Saul's failure and to anoint David as his successor.

Where do we see Jesus in this passage?

The human yearning for godly leadership can only be fulfilled in the King of kings, Jesus Christ. All other, earthly rulers will let us down. The best they can do is make us yearn all the more for the coming of Christ. Jesus presently reigns as Head of his church and one day will reign over all the earth.

The human yearning for godly leadership can only be fulfilled in the King of kings, Jesus Christ. All other, earthly rulers will let us down.

Jesus is the King with perfect integrity, fulfilling all that was required of kings in Israel (Deut. 17:14–20) while being guilty of none of the corruption against which Samuel warned (8:11–17). Rather than taking from his people and running up debt, Jesus is the King who gives to his people by removing our debt of sin and enriching us with his righteousness (2 Cor. 8:9; Mark 10:45). In contrast to greedy earthly rulers, Jesus's yoke is easy and his burden is light (Matt. 11:28–30). Jesus is also the King who has fought our battles (1 Sam. 8:20), winning the final victory over sin and death. Though the majority may have rejected him (John 1:11; 19:15), he doesn't need their votes. One day he will return to judge his enemies and bless his people. He will reign forever (Rev. 21:1–5). May our King come again soon!

How does this passage apply to us?

- Few passages in the Old Testament are more directly relevant to the world in which we live. We look to mere human beings as saviors, whether in the realm of the nation or the church. "Cursed is the man who trusts in mankind and makes flesh his strength, and whose heart turns away from the LORD. For he will be like a bush in the desert and will not see when prosperity comes, but will live in stony wastes in the wilderness" (Jer. 17:5–6). Just as the people of Israel believed they needed a king to make them secure, so people today wrongfully put their ultimate trust in politicians. Francis Schaeffer warned that people will give up their freedom in order to gain personal peace and affluence.[1] Politicians campaign as messiahs, promising to meet every need and to usher in an age of prosperity and peace in a new world order or a great society. R. C. Sproul warns against statism, which is a philosophy of government in which the state is not only the final ruling authority, but also the agency of redemption.[2] When we look to government to solve all our problems of disease, poverty, education, care for the elderly, patronage of the arts, and the elimination of prejudice, we will sacrifice our economic and personal freedoms, just as Samuel warned Israel (8:11–18).

> The more we demand from government, the more power we must give it.

The more we demand from government, the more power we must give it. Sadly, the people don't get what they have bargained for. It was observed by Lord Acton that "Power tends to corrupt, and absolute power corrupts absolutely."[3] Taxes are raised. Money is wasted. Influence is purchased either directly through bribes or indirectly through campaign contributions. Problems are not solved and often get worse.

- The church also has a history of looking to human leadership when it should look to Christ. Jesus is the sole head of his universal church (Eph. 2:22; 5:23; Col. 1:18), with each local church being led by a plurality of mutually accountable elders/overseers/pastors under Christ (Acts 14:23; Titus 1:5; 1 Tim. 5:17). When the church strays from the biblical structure by concentrating all the power in the church in one man, corruption results (3 John 1:9), as the focus veers away from Christ onto the human leader. When churches have created extra-biblical offices in which men rule over many churches, even more corruption has taken place. Sometimes the people of God may say, as did the Israelites, "Why can't we be like all the other churches and have a dynamic strong leader who will help us to grow large?" Perhaps we could offer a warning like that of Samuel: "They will take the best of your men for their denominational boards; they will ordain your daughters as pastors; they will seize your church property; they will take the best of your tithes for their denominational bureaucracy. Then you will cry out because of the denomination you have chosen for yourselves." Christ Jesus is the Chief Shepherd (1 Peter 5:4), under whom his undershepherds serve in local churches. We cannot give to human leaders the headship which belongs to Christ alone.

- We should learn from the failure of our leaders that we can trust in God alone. "Blessed is the man who trusts in the LORD and whose trust is the LORD. For he will be like a tree planted by the water, that extends its roots by a stream and will not fear when the heat comes; but its leaves will be green, and it will not be anxious in a year of drought nor cease to yield fruit" (Jer. 17:7–8).
- Our passage also illustrates the truth that majority rule does not always produce the right result. The majority in Israel wrongly wanted a king. A majority can be wrong or even engage in tyranny. The majority in a nation may wrongfully favor Islamic sharia law—which includes the execution of converts to Christianity—or homosexual marriage, or abortion on demand. The majority in a church may want women pastors, be against the practice of church discipline, or favor entertainment in worship so that the church can be more like the outside world. The voice of the people, however, is not the voice of God. Ultimate authority rests with him alone.

FOR FURTHER STUDY

1. Why did Samuel's sons, like those of Eli, turn out badly? (See 1 Sam. 2:29; 8:3; Prov. 29:15.)
2. Does the Bible teach that believing parents should expect all their children to be godly?
3. How often in Scripture do godly parents have ungodly children? How often do we see cases of multi-generational faith (Ezek. 18:5–32; Luke 12:52)?
4. Does the Bible teach a particular form of civil government?
5. What is the biblical view of the role of human government (1 Peter 2:13–17; Rom. 13:1–7)? What is government to do? What limitations, if any, are to be put on its power?

TO THINK ABOUT AND DISCUSS

1. Given that the Lord had previously revealed that Israel would one day have kings (Deut. 17:14–20), why was it wrong for the Israelites to ask for a king?
2. Why did the Lord give in to the people's wrong desire for a king?
3. How are we tempted to look to human deliverers or heroes in politics or in the church, instead of looking to God?
4. What are the dangers of big government (civil and ecclesiastical)?
5. How does this passage point to Christ?

6 Saul, the people's king, leads Israel

(9:1–11:15)

The people have demanded a king who will lead them into battle, so the Lord gives them the king for whom they have asked. While Saul is initially hesitant to assume the throne, his reign gets off to a good start when he successfully leads Israel into battle against the Ammonites and delivers the city of Jabesh-gilead.

Saul looks for donkeys and finds a kingdom (9:1–10:27)

Saul is introduced as a man from an important family of the tribe of Benjamin. He looks like a king, being the tallest and handsomest among the sons of Israel (9:1–2). Contemporary studies have shown that in politics, the taller, better-looking candidates tend to win elections. If American football had been played in Israel, Saul would have been team captain and All-American. This is the man whom the people of Israel have been seeking to lead them. His name even means "asked for."

As we are introduced to Saul, however, some concerns

come to mind. One is that Jacob had prophesied that the kings of Israel would come from Judah (Gen. 49:10), which implies that Saul is unlikely to establish a dynasty. Also, the emphasis upon Saul's outward appearance is in contrast to what is later said about how God sees people: "Do not look at his appearance or at the height of his stature, because I have rejected him; for God sees not as man sees, for man looks at the outward appearance, but the LORD looks at the heart" (1 Sam. 16:7).

When we first meet Saul, he is searching for his father's lost donkeys. When Saul and his servant can't find the donkeys, the servant suggests that they go to the man of God, who may be able to use his prophetic powers to help them find the missing animals. Saul's servant says of Samuel, "All that he says surely comes true" (9:6). Little does Saul know what Samuel will say, far beyond the matter of his donkeys, and how this encounter with Samuel will forever change his life (9:3–14).

The Lord has already told Samuel that the future king will be coming to see him: "About this time tomorrow I will send you a man from the land of Benjamin, and you shall anoint him to be prince over My people Israel; and he will deliver My people from the hand of the Philistines" (9:16). The sequence of events which brings Saul to Samuel have been orchestrated by the Lord. God is sovereign over donkeys and where they wander, and over the movements of Saul and his servant in searching for them.

I am God, and there is no other.
I am God, and there is no one like Me,
Declaring the end from the beginning,

And from ancient times things which have not been done,
Saying, "My purpose will be established,
And I will accomplish all My good pleasure";
Calling a bird of prey from the east,
The man of My purpose from a far country.
Truly I have spoken; truly I will bring it to pass.
I have planned it, surely I will do it.

(Isa. 46:9–11)

God also gives Samuel the job description of the new king, which is to deliver Israel from its enemies, in answer to the request of the people (see 8:20).

When Samuel and Saul meet, the prophet first demonstrates his divine knowledge by telling Saul that the donkeys have been found. Then, with the same prophetic authority, Samuel reveals something much more important: the Lord has great purposes for Saul (9:18–20). Saul replies with what seems to be a mixture of humility and bewilderment that the prophet would say such things about him (9:21). Some suggest that Saul's response to Samuel here is one of unbelief and foreshadows the coming troubles of this fleshly king. This view is supported by the fact that it is not Saul but his servant who thinks of turning to the Lord through his prophet for help. Saul seems to be ignorant of who Samuel is, even though all Israel knows about him (3:20).

Samuel gives a banquet in Saul's honor, after which Samuel speaks with Saul and anoints him as the king of Israel (9:22–10:1). Anointing signified the consecration or setting apart of a man to God's service, which could be as prophet, priest, or king. Later, Samuel would anoint David (16:12–13). David would refuse to harm Saul because of his respect for him as one anointed by God (24:6, 10; 26:9, 11). We get our English word "Messiah" from the Hebrew word translated "anoint." Those who were anointed under the Old Covenant looked ahead to the Christ, the Anointed One (2:10).

Samuel implicitly reminds Saul that, as king, he remains under God's authority, and that Israel is the Lord's possession. Samuel then instructs Saul concerning remarkable events which will further confirm that the Lord has set him apart as king over Israel (10:2–8). Samuel's prediction of whom Saul will encounter and what they will say again demonstrates God's sovereign control over all things. The most significant sign is that the Spirit will come upon Saul, transforming him and demonstrating to others that God has equipped him to serve as king. Saul obeys Samuel and all that was predicted comes to pass (10:9–13). When Saul returns home, he apparently doesn't tell his family about the amazing things which have happened to him. His anointing remains a secret.

Samuel then calls the people of Israel together at Mizpah so that Saul can be publicly chosen as king (10:17–19). Again the prophet reminds the people of the Lord's faithfulness to them and their wickedness in demanding a king. Then, out of all the tribes of Israel, Saul is miraculously chosen by lot (10:20–21). Under the Old Covenant, the Lord sometimes guided his people through the casting of lots (Deut. 17:15; Prov. 16:33). Lots were used in, for example, the choosing of a scapegoat and in the apportionment of the land (Lev. 16:8–10; Num. 26:53–56; Josh. 7:18). The last time lots are used in the Bible is when the apostles choose Matthias as a replacement for Judas (Acts 1:26). We are not sure exactly how the lots looked or worked, but like the rolling of dice or the tossing of a coin they produced an apparently random result which proved to be God's decision for the people.

This casting of lots is the second of three confirmations that Saul is to be king, the first being his private anointing by Samuel. Saul, however, hides from the people, perhaps overwhelmed by the responsibility (10:22; his shyness is in sharp contrast to the attitude of today's politicians, who do all they can to gain high office). When the people see Saul's impressive outward appearance they acclaim their new king (10:23–24). Samuel writes out the regulations for the king, reminding him and the people that the king's authority is not absolute, but that he is subject to God and his law (Deut. 17:14–20). Then everyone, including Saul, returns home (10:25–26). While many valiant men follow Saul, there is still an element of "worthless men" (10:27; the same term is used of Eli's evil sons at 2:12) who do not acknowledge Saul's reign.

King Saul delivers Israel from the Ammonites (11:1–15)

The Ammonites, like the Philistines, are neighboring enemies of Israel. Unlike the Philistines, however, the Ammonites were related to Israel through Abraham's nephew, Lot (Gen. 19:38). Nahash, the Ammonite king, is terrorizing Israel. He has besieged the city of Jabesh-gilead, which has offered to conditionally surrender (v. 1). Nahash's terms are harsh: he demands their mutilation (gouging out their right eyes) and humiliation (v. 2). The elders of Jabesh desperately need a deliverer (vv. 3–4), which gives Saul the opportunity to prove that he is a worthy king. The Spirit of God comes upon Saul, who is filled with holy anger (vv. 5–6). Saul summons the men of Israel to fight for their brethren in Jabesh. The cutting up of the oxen and sending the pieces throughout the land is a dramatic call to battle. A similar method was used in the days of the judges (Judg. 19:29).

Saul calls the men forth in his name as king and also in the name of Samuel, the acknowledged prophet (v. 7), and the men of war respond to his leadership (v. 8). He sends good news of coming deliverance to the men of Jabesh, who deliver their own cryptic message to the Ammonites (vv. 9–10; "We will come out to you" would sound to the Ammonites as if the men of Jabesh were coming out to submit to them, but instead it would prove to mean "we will come out to fight you"). Saul, employing sound military strategy, then leads Israel to a great victory over the Ammonites, thus proving himself to be a worthy king (v. 11). Saul further demonstrates his worthiness by giving glory to God and by showing mercy to his detractors in Israel (vv. 12–13). Samuel then leads the people in a third acknowledgment of Saul as king, and Israel celebrates with offerings before the Lord (vv. 14–15). The reign of the people's king is off to a great start.

Where do we see Jesus in this passage?

Jesus is the King chosen by God (10:24; Isa. 42:1). He is the Anointed One (10:1; Isa. 61:1; Luke 4:18). He is empowered by the Holy Spirit (10:6; 11:6; Matt. 3:16; Isa. 61:1–3). In contrast to Saul, the people's choice, Jesus was not outwardly attractive to humankind (9:2; 10:23–24; Isa. 53:1–3). Yet Jesus is the one who is wonderful beyond comparison (S. of S. 5:10). Jesus, like Saul, was silent before his detractors and did not retaliate against them (10:27; Isa. 53:7; 1 Peter 2:23).

Just as Saul's kingship was concealed for a season before being fully revealed, so Jesus's royal majesty is still hidden to many (10:16; Luke 18:34). Just as some embraced Saul as God's anointed king while others rejected him, so some have received Jesus while worthless men rejected him because he was not the kind of king they were seeking (10:26–27; John 1:11–13). Just as Saul was angered by the evil done by the enemies of the Lord, so Jesus was righteously angered by evil (11:6; John 2:14–17; Mark 3:5). Just as Saul brought deliverance to the besieged people of Jabesh, so Jesus brings deliverance from the terrible oppression and reproach of sin and death to those who cry out to him (11:5–11; Isa. 25:8; 1 Cor. 15:55–57). Just as Saul's kingdom was established through his victory over the Ammonites, so Jesus's kingdom is established as a result of his victory over Satan, sin, and death (Heb. 2:8; Rom. 1:4).

How does this passage apply to us?

- Just as God controlled the donkeys in their getting lost, not being found by Saul, and then returning home on their own, all to achieve God's purpose of bringing Saul to Samuel, so God controls all things today for his good purposes. Every event in nature, every detail of history, even the free choices of other people: all are part of the sovereign plan of the one "who works all things after the counsel of His will" (Eph. 1:11). There are significant examples of God's providence in church history; for example, when Calvin sought to merely pass through Geneva and ended up being persuaded by Farel to remain in the city, which then became the center of Calvin's life's work. We can also reflect, with thanksgiving, on how God has providentially guided our paths until now. Each of us can look back upon the events which led to our conversion. I marvel when I think of all the circumstances which led to my marriage, including the decisions of both sets of parents to live in a certain neighborhood in Dallas, our choices of where to go to college, our participating in the school band, and so on. The same can be done when I think of how our church was established, how the Lord gave us a building in which to meet, how he brought together our present group of elders, how he allowed us to get involved in vital missions projects, and so on. God still works out his extraordinary purposes through seemingly ordinary circumstances. For example, God leads a troubled woman to faith after a friend encourages her to seek biblical counsel through a local church. This woman is converted, becomes involved in the life of the church, and ends up in a blessed marriage to one of the pastors.

Understanding God's providence also helps us to realize that even the hard things in our past were not tragic accidents but part of his perfect plan.

- Understanding God's providence also helps us to realize that even the hard things in our past were not tragic accidents but part of his perfect plan. "And we know that God causes all things to work together for good to those who love God, to those who are called according to His purpose" (Rom. 8:28). The truth of God's sovereignty also gives us hope for the future. No harm can come to us unless it is part of God's plan for his own glory and our good. Nothing can separate us from his love for us (Rom. 8:38–39).

- Does the fact that God works through the events in our lives mean that we should be trying to interpret our circumstances as signs from God? "The secret things belong to the LORD our God, but the things revealed belong to us and to our sons forever, that we may observe all the words of this law" (Deut. 29:29). Saul's father, Saul himself, his servant, and the donkeys were not at all aware that they were being led by God. We cannot know the secret purposes God has for the present and future events in our lives. Just as Saul needed a word from the prophet in order to understand what God was doing in his life (9:27), so our focus should be on what God has revealed to us in his Word, which will help us to know how to respond to our circumstances in a way that pleases him.
- The Lord revealed his choice of Saul through the casting of lots (10:20–21). Should we make major decisions, such as choosing church leaders, in the same manner? While it is true that the apostles chose the replacement for Judas by casting lots (Acts 1:26), they did not cast lots for just anyone among them, but only for those who met the qualifications of being men who had been with Jesus from the beginning. Later, when Paul gives instructions for the choosing of church leaders, he gives lists of qualifications by which the church can know whom God has chosen to be elders or deacons (1 Tim. 3:1–13), while making no mention of the casting of lots. Nor are there any instructions in the New

Testament for making decisions in this way. God guides us through his Word. Unlike those under the Old Covenant, we are blessed to have the completed canon of Scripture by which we can know the Lord's will.

- The Lord made it clear that Saul's authority was not absolute, for even the king is subject to the Lord (10:25). In the same way our political leaders are under God's authority. If they ever call us to do what is wrong, we must obey God rather than them (Acts 5:29). The authority of husbands and parents is also granted by God and under his authority. Our church leaders are likewise under the authority of Christ, the Chief Shepherd and Head of the church, which is his possession purchased by his blood (1 Peter 5:4; Acts 20:28). We have no right to go beyond Scripture in the use of our offices.
- As we continue to read Saul's story, we will see that, after a good start, Saul stops submitting to God's law and becomes a murderous despot. His downfall should serve as a warning to all who would lead.
- Saul had righteous anger at the enemies of God (11:6), but later is consumed by sinful anger (20:30, 33). Righteous anger, fueled by a zeal for God's glory, is rare; which is why James warns us to be slow to anger (James 1:19; Prov. 14:29; 25:28).
- While God gives victory in battle, Saul exerts effort and employs tactics (11:11). In our spiritual warfare we acknowledge that we are completely dependent upon God, but we also are responsible for striving for victory and employing wise strategies.

For further study ▶

FOR FURTHER STUDY

1. Where in the Bible do we see examples of God's sovereign hand guiding the free acts of people? See Proverbs 21:1; Isaiah 46:9–11; Acts 2:23; Genesis 50:20.
2. Is there ever a time today, under the New Covenant, when we should cast lots when making decisions, with the expectation that the Lord will guide us?
3. What was the significance of anointing someone in the Old Testament? Is there any New Testament use of anointing?
4. How do modern tyrants compare with Nahash the Ammonite (11:1–2)? Are we more civilized today?

TO THINK ABOUT AND DISCUSS

1. How has God's sovereign providence brought blessing into your life?
2. If God works out his purposes through circumstances in our lives, should we interpret open doors and opportunities as his guidance?
3. How does the selection and function of our church leaders compare with the selection and function of the kings of Israel?
4. What is the nature of our warfare under the New Covenant (Eph. 6:12–20)?
5. In what ways is King Saul like King Jesus, and in what ways does he differ from our Lord?

7 Saul's failure and folly

(13:1–15:35)

Saul's reign has such a hopeful beginning as he humbly accepts the responsibility of serving as Israel's king. He then proves his worthiness by delivering the people of Jabesh from the Ammonites, while giving glory to God. His popularity among the people is soaring. Sadly, Saul now turns from the Lord, setting his will over God's will.

While we enjoy learning from the good examples in the Bible, such as Joseph, Ruth, or Daniel, God also teaches us through people like Saul who fail miserably. If Hebrews 11 is considered to be a "Hall of Fame" for great heroes whose faith we ought to imitate, men like Saul belong in a "Hall of Shame" of bad examples. We can benefit from his example so that we will not fall into the same sins (1 Cor. 10:11).

Saul fails a test in his war with the Philistines (13:1–23)

Seeking to fulfill his mandate to fight the enemies of Israel,

Saul goes to war against the Philistines, who are oppressing God's people (vv. 1–7). We are introduced to Saul's son, Jonathan, who strikes a blow against the Philistine garrison, after which the Philistines mobilize with plans to retaliate with overwhelming force (vv. 3–4). The people of Israel are terrified, but Saul tries to rally the troops for battle.

Saul now faces a test. He has been told by Samuel to wait until he arrives before going into battle (v. 8; see 10:8). But the prophet isn't on time, and Saul's small army is scattering, perhaps to join their countrymen in hiding from the Philistines (v. 8b, 6). Finally, Saul takes it upon himself to go ahead and offer the sacrifices, seeking God's blessing upon the battle, without Samuel (v. 9). Just then the prophet arrives (v. 10). While we might sympathize with Saul's plight, Samuel's delay is a test of Saul's faithfulness to God. He has disobeyed God's Word through Samuel (vv. 8, 13). He also appears to have overstepped his kingly office by performing sacrificial functions reserved for priests, although some commentators suggest that Saul may have offered the sacrifice through priests. They also point out that David and Solomon are said to have offered up sacrifices (perhaps through priests) without being condemned (2 Sam. 24:25; 1 Kings 3:4, 15; 8:63). Nevertheless, this incident reminds us of proud King Uzziah, who usurped the priestly function by burning incense in the temple (2 Chr. 26:16–21).

Saul's root sin is unbelief. He trusts in his own reasoning rather than submitting to God (Prov. 3:5–6). He sees his army breaking up and determines that this emergency justifies violating God's Word, believing that it is better to offend God than to lose followers. When confronted with his sin by

Samuel, Saul offers many excuses (vv. 11–12), which further compounds his guilt. He blames the people for scattering, and Samuel for being late. He claims that the situation with the Philistines has made it necessary for him to act quickly. He even suggests that he meant well, in that he was seeking God's favor before going into battle.

Saul has committed a tragic, life-altering sin. He should have trusted the Lord and waited on him, remembering that the God who enabled Gideon to conquer with an army of three hundred men could help him to defeat the Philistines even with a small army.

The prophet Samuel rebukes Saul and pronounces judgment upon him. Because of his disobedience, Saul's dynasty will not endure. The Lord has determined to replace him with a better man, a man after God's own heart (vv. 13–14). After this, the oppression of Israel by the Philistines becomes even more intense (vv. 15–23). Saul has only a tiny army and almost no weapons. The people are worse off than ever before. Their tall, handsome king has failed them.

Saul foolishly undermines Jonathan's victory over the Philistines (14:1–52)

While Saul seems to be hunkered down avoiding battle, his son, Jonathan, formulates an audacious secret plan to mount a surprise attack against the Philistines (vv. 1–10). Showing bravery and a great trust in God, which will later characterize David in his fight with Goliath, Jonathan declares, "Come and let us cross over to the garrison of these uncircumcised; perhaps the LORD will work for us, for the LORD is not restrained to save by many or by few" (v. 6). After Jonathan strikes a mighty blow against the Philistines (vv. 11–15), Saul and the rest of the army join the battle (vv. 16–22). The Lord receives glory for delivering his people, showing that they can overcome overwhelming odds against them when they trust in him (v. 23).

The extent of Jonathan's victory is severely limited, however, when King Saul makes a foolish and vain vow that none of his men are to eat on the day of battle. Because the army is deprived of the strengthening food it needs to press home its advantage, the Philistines are able to escape (vv. 25–30). Jonathan, who has not heard about Saul's vow, tastes some honey during the battle (v. 27). Saul, in his arrogant folly, seeks to put Jonathan to death, but the people insist that he live, in light of the great deliverance Jonathan has brought about that day (vv. 36–46). Saul, having missed his opportunity for total victory, continues to wage war against Israel's enemies (vv. 47–52).

Saul fails again in his war against the Amalekites (15:1–35)

Saul is given one final opportunity to serve and obey the Lord when he is instructed by Samuel to utterly destroy the Amalekites (vv. 1–3). Because of their past and present sins, the Amalekites are under God's just wrath. The Lord has determined to blot them out from under heaven (Exod. 17:8–16; Num. 24:20; Deut. 25:17–19).

Many people today are offended by the slaughter of the Amalekites. Some even claim that this text is not inspired but reflects the primitive religion of the Hebrews, who believed in a God of wrath instead of our more advanced concept of

God as love. They fail to understand that God righteously judges the wicked who foolishly oppose him and his people. While we are not authorized to take personal revenge, vengeance does belong to the Lord (Rom. 12:19). Those who are offended by this account also fail to grasp the sinfulness of mankind (Rom. 3:10–20). The Amalekites deserved what they got. Rather than asking, "How could a God of love act in this way?" a better question might be, "Why did the Lord put up with these wicked Amalekites for so long?" We also learn that, even when punishment is delayed, God will bring judgment. This is true both of nations and of individuals (Heb. 9:27).

While we are not authorized to take personal revenge, vengeance does belong to the Lord.

Saul is again being tested, as Samuel's instructions are specific. This is not a war of conquest from which the Israelites are to take away captives and property. The Amalekites are to be totally destroyed, like Jericho (Josh. 6:17, 21). Saul should have remembered what happened to Achan when he tried to keep some of the spoils from Jericho (Josh. 7:17–26).

Saul summons the army and leads them in victory over the Amalekites, but again he fails the test when he spares Agag, their king, and allows the people to keep the best of the spoils of war which the Lord had devoted to destruction (15:4–9). Ancient rulers would sometimes spare the kings of the nations they conquered so that they could keep them around as trophies or royal slaves to commemorate the greatness of the conqueror. Saul was acting like the kings of the surrounding nations rather than being the unique holy king of the people of God. His problem with the Lord's command was different from ours. He didn't mind killing a bunch of Amalekites. His objection was that he didn't want to destroy the valuable spoils of war.

The Lord is grieved by Saul's disobedience and sends Samuel, who is also grieved, to rebuke the king (vv. 10–19). The biblical concept of God being grieved, or repenting, is somewhat mysterious (also see Gen. 6:5–6). God controls all things by his changeless decree (Eph. 1:11) and does not change his mind (1 Sam. 15:29; Mal. 3:6). Yet in his involvement with humanity he is genuinely grieved over human sin; for example, Jesus wept over Jerusalem (Luke 19:41–44). In this case, we know that the Lord's ultimate plan was that David from the tribe of Judah would become the king in place of Saul and his dynasty would never end (Gen. 49:10; 2 Sam. 8:15).

Saul seems oblivious to his sin, claiming to have done the Lord's will (v. 13). Then, when confronted with the evidence of his defiance of the Lord's command, Saul again makes excuses, claiming that partial obedience is enough, blaming the people for taking the spoil, and stating that the animals had been kept for sacrifice to the Lord (vv. 20–21). Samuel rebukes Saul's expediency, saying that obedience is more important than sacrifice and that disobedience is no better than idolatrous pagan worship (vv. 22–23a). As a consequence, Saul's kingdom is to be taken away (v. 23b).

Upon hearing this pronouncement of judgment, Saul pleads for pardon, but it quickly becomes apparent that he is more concerned about saving face before the people, by appearing to have Samuel's support, than repenting before God (vv. 24–31). When Saul tears Samuel's robe, Samuel states that this is symbolic of God tearing his kingdom away from him and giving it to a better man (vv. 27–29). Samuel finishes the job Saul failed to do by carrying out the Lord's judgment on the Amalekite king (vv. 32–33). Finally, Samuel parts from Saul, which appears to symbolize that the prophet and the Lord are done with this failed king (vv. 34–35).

Saul, the king for whom the people asked, began well by fighting Israel's enemies. But he was a proud, fleshly man who was not careful to fear and obey the Lord. Because of this, the Lord determined to take away his kingdom. As we continue in 1 Samuel, Saul sinks further into arrogance, pride, and godlessness, until finally the Lord removes him.

Where do we see Jesus in this passage?

Jesus is a kind of anti-Saul. He obeyed God the Father perfectly, even unto death, and wasn't concerned about the approval of men (John 15:10; 8:29). He faced the greatest imaginable temptation to sin, but acted wisely, remaining faithful to his calling (Matt. 4:1–11; Luke 22:39–46; Heb. 5:7–8). When we are sorely tempted we can call upon him, knowing that he sympathizes with us and comes to our aid (Heb. 4:16). Unlike Saul, who lost his kingdom because of his sinful failure, Jesus, through his perfect obedience, has gained an everlasting kingdom (Rev. 11:15). God will never "regret" making Jesus King (1 Sam. 15:11; Ps. 89:29). Jesus grieves over the sinful disobedience of people (1 Sam. 15:11; Luke 19:41–44). When Saul failed, the Lord promised a king who would be better than Saul, a reference to David in the short term, who was a type of Jesus, the one who will be King forever (1 Sam. 15:28). God commands all people everywhere to submit to him by believing in his Son (Acts 17:30). Those who refuse will, like the Amalekites, be utterly destroyed under God's wrath (Matt. 13:41–42, 47–50).

Jesus is seen positively in the exploits of Jonathan. Jesus fought our enemy, not merely risking his life, but giving his life to win the victory. Just as the faithfulness of Jonathan inspired others to follow him into battle, so Jesus's victory inspires us to follow him.

How does this passage apply to us?

- Saul's rapid decline should be a warning to us all, especially those who aspire to leadership. As was the case with the sons of Eli and Samuel, Saul illustrates how human nature can be corrupted when handling power. Actually, it is not power which corrupts: power merely reveals the corruption inside a person (Mark 7:18–23). In the same way, our political leaders, who take office with high ideals, are often like the very people against whom they campaigned.
- Church leaders also can be tempted by power. Men who were once used by God have fallen into sins of pride, anger, greed, and immorality. Church leaders, like Saul, can be tempted to please their congregations rather than God because they fear losing members. We need leaders who fear God and not men and women (Prov. 29:25). Paul warns, "Let him who thinks he stands take heed that he does not fall" (1 Cor. 10:12). Paul also offers hope and comfort: "No temptation has overtaken you but such as is

common to man; and God is faithful, who will not allow you to be tempted beyond what you are able, but with the temptation will provide the way of escape also, so that you will be able to endure it" (1 Cor. 10:13). Christian leaders do not have to fall into Saul's sins. With God's help they can remain faithful to their calling.

- We also learn that it is important to obey the Lord. While it is true that we are saved by Christ's obedience and not our own, those who know and love Christ will obey him (John 14:15). We, like Saul, may be tested when God's Word tells us to do things which don't seem to make sense, or when the Lord allows circumstances in which it is very hard to do the right thing. Just as Samuel's delay tested Saul's faithfulness (13:8), so our faith may be tested. For example, a single woman who longs to be married may be tempted to settle for an unbelieving man, contrary to God's Word (1 Cor. 7:39; 9:5). She must learn to trust the Lord and to wait on him (Ps. 33:20; 130:5; James 5:7).

While it is true that we are saved by Christ's obedience and not our own, those who know and love Christ will obey him.

- Saul's failure to fully carry out the Lord's command to wipe out the Amalekites reminds us that our obedience is to be complete. We can't pick and choose which of God's commands we will follow. Partial obedience involves disobedience and does not please the Lord.
- We, like Saul, who blamed the people both for his premature sacrifice and for his failure to completely

carry out God's judgment on Amalek, can be tempted to rationalize our sin by blaming others or even God (James 1:13). A husband has an affair and blames his wife, because she isn't meeting his needs. Children use the sin and hypocrisy of their parents as an excuse for being disrespectful and disobedient. Such thinking is practical atheism because it leaves God out of the picture.

- Nor should we fall into Saul's sins of expediency. Saul thought that he had no choice but to go ahead and offer the sacrifice. He feared the consequences of waiting (13:9). The pregnant single woman may contemplate having an abortion, claiming that she has no choice if she is to complete her education. A woman may divorce her husband without biblical grounds because she thinks that she must be free to express herself. The student cheats on the test because he has to make a good grade.
- Just as Saul's sacrifices were unacceptable to God because of his disobedience (13:9; 15:22–23), so our external religious acts without heartfelt obedience are worthless (Matt. 15:9–10).
- Saul's foolish oath (14:24) also warns us against making rash vows (Matt. 5:33–37). We should be very careful—"slow to speak" (James 1:19)—before making any promises. We should also test our motives for making such promises.
- Saul's downfall is a reminder that you can never defy God and win. Your sin will find you out, and what you sow you will also reap (Num. 32:23; Gal. 6:7–8). Many of our troubles, like those of Saul, are of our own making, the consequences of leaning on our own understanding rather

than trusting the Lord. On the other hand, God promises blessing to those who trust and obey him, especially when we follow his ways in difficult circumstances. He will make our paths straight (Prov. 3:6).

- On a more positive note, Jonathan's great victory, against all human odds, encourages us to trust in God and not to fear other people. Our battles are not military encounters with Philistines; we are engaged in spiritual warfare (Eph. 6:11–12). Though the lost seem to be hardened in their unbelief, we can boldly evangelize them, scaling spiritual cliffs, knowing that nothing is impossible with God (1 Sam. 14:6).
- Jonathan's victory also illustrates how one person with audacious faith can inspire others to follow. Great movements in missions have begun with one visionary leader through whom God has moved many to serve him.

For further study ▶

FOR FURTHER STUDY

1. How was God's command to slaughter the Amalekites just?
2. What similar manifestations of God's wrath are found in Scripture? How do these typify the final judgment?
3. What other foolish vows do we read of in Scripture? See, for example, Judges 11:30–40 and Matthew 14:6–12.
4. Is there ever a time when a vow should be broken because it was made sinfully and because that sin would be compounded by keeping the vow?
5. How can it be that godly fathers like Eli and Samuel had ungodly sons, while ungodly Saul had a godly son, Jonathan?

TO THINK ABOUT AND DISCUSS

1. When can we, like Saul, be tempted to rationalize our disobedience to God?
2. Why is it so hard for leaders to remain humble and godly?
3. If the Lord is in control of all things, including the choice of Saul as king, in what sense could he "regret" having made Saul king (15:10)?
4. Contrast what we know about the characters of Jonathan and Saul.
5. How can we imitate Jonathan's bold faith (14:6)?
6. Is there ever a time when you should make an oath or a vow?
7. Where can we see Christ in these chapters?

8 The Lord anoints David as his king

(16:1–23)

A major theme of 1 Samuel is Israel's need for a righteous leader. Both Eli and Samuel failed to produce a worthy dynasty. The people then asked for a king, and in Saul they got exactly what they asked for, and perhaps what they deserved.

Saul was a man of impressive outward appearance who seemed well suited to lead his people to victory over their enemies. But Saul, the people's choice, proved by his self-willed disobedience of the Lord that he was not a worthy king for Israel. The Lord declared through Samuel, "Because you have rejected the word of the LORD, He has also rejected you from being king" (15:23). The Lord also promised to raise up a better king in Saul's place: "The LORD has sought out for Himself a man after His own heart, and the LORD has appointed him as ruler over His people, because you have not kept what the LORD has commanded you" (13:14). "The LORD has torn the kingdom of Israel from you today and has given it to your neighbor, who is better than you" (15:28).

We have now come to the crucial chapter in which the Lord makes his choice of the man who will be Israel's king, through whom he will create a dynasty culminating in the Messiah, who will reign forever. For the rest of 1 Samuel we will observe the rise of David, the Lord's chosen one, and the decline of the people's choice, Saul.

God looks at the heart (vv. 1–13)

The Lord tells the prophet Samuel that the time has come to anoint a king to replace Saul and he instructs him to go to the house of Jesse to anoint this new king from among his sons. Jesse was the grandson of Boaz and Ruth (Ruth 4:13–22) and was from the tribe of Judah, from which Jacob had prophesied that Israel's kings would come (Gen. 49:10). Jesse's obscure home village of Bethlehem would become famous for the rest of history as the city of David and later the birthplace of Jesus. Unlike Saul, who was the king the people demanded, this new king is one about whom the Lord says, "I have selected [him] for Myself" (16:1). This new king will be a different kind of king.

While the fact that the Lord is working out his plan should be taken as good news, Samuel is fearful. "How can I go? When Saul hears of it, he will kill me" (v. 2a). Saul, who himself is guilty of treason against the Lord, has become a godless tyrant who is willing to execute even a prophet if he suspects treason against his kingdom. Later, he will actually murder the Lord's priests (22:19). The Lord instructs Samuel to tell Saul that he is going to offer sacrifices in Bethlehem, but

Samuel does not reveal to Saul the occasion of the sacrifice, which is the anointing of a new king (vv. 2b–3).

When Samuel arrives in Bethlehem, the people are afraid that he has come in judgment, but the prophet assures them that he has come in peace. He invites Jesse and his sons to the sacrifice (vv. 4–5).

As Jesse's sons are brought before him, Samuel is impressed by Eliab's stature (v. 6). This man, like Saul, looks like a king. Later, we will see that Eliab's character is also fleshly like that of Saul (17:28). The Lord corrects Samuel, saying, "Do not look at his appearance or at the height of his stature, because I have rejected him; for God sees not as man sees, for man looks at the outward appearance, but the LORD looks at the heart" (v. 7). God knows our true natures: our thoughts, our characters, our motives, and our desires (Ps. 139).

God knows our true natures: our thoughts, our characters, our motives, and our desires.

Six other sons of Jesse pass before Samuel, but none of these is the chosen one (vv. 8–10). Samuel, realizing that the Lord must have chosen a son who is not present, asks Jesse if he has another son. Jesse reveals that there is one more, the youngest son, who is out tending sheep. We are not told why David is not initially present when the prophet calls, but we suspect that it is because he is regarded as the least among Jesse's offspring, a man in whom Samuel would have no interest. Samuel insists that David be summoned at once from the fields (v. 11).

When David arrives, it turns out that his outward appearance is also handsome (v. 12), but this is not why he is chosen. The Lord says to Samuel, "Arise, anoint him; for this is he" (v. 12), so the prophet pours oil over David, anointing him as Israel's future king. The Spirit of the Lord then comes mightily upon David, empowering him for the work he is to undertake (v. 13). While the Spirit had also come upon Saul (10:10) only to later depart from him (16:14), the Spirit will remain with David (Ps. 51:11; 2 Sam. 23:2).

The psalmist Asaph describes this scene:

He also chose David His servant
And took him from the sheepfolds.
From the care of the ewes with suckling lambs He brought him
To shepherd Jacob His people,
And Israel His inheritance.
So he shepherded them according to the integrity of his heart,
And guided them with skillful hands.

(Ps. 78:70–73)

David's early life as a shepherd has prepared him for being king. He has learned how to fight with the Lord's help when he has taken on the lion and the bear when they have attacked his sheep (17:34–37). His loving care of his flock will be reflected in his care for his subjects in Israel.

We are not told how David, his father, and his brothers respond to these remarkable events. Apparently, David goes back to his sheep (v. 19) and his anointing remains a secret to Saul and the people of Israel. David's position as God's chosen future king is a dangerous one, because of Saul's murderous pride. Rather than actively pursuing the throne,

David waits upon the Lord's timing for the fulfillment of Samuel's prophecy.

David enters Saul's service (vv. 14–23)

The first record of David participating in the public life of Israel occurs when Saul brings him into the court to play his harp. When God judges Saul for his disobedience by removing his Spirit and sending an evil spirit to terrorize him (vv. 14–15), Saul's servants recommend that a man be brought to play the harp so that Saul can have some relief (vv. 16–17). We are not told what it is about the music that soothes Saul. Elsewhere, music is tied to spiritual activity (10:5; 2 Kings 3:15; 1 Chr. 13:8; Ps. 33:2–3). Not all music, however, is worship (Amos 5:23).

One servant knows about David's musical skill, so David is summoned to play for the king (vv. 18–20). David gains the king's favor and is invited to remain at court (vv. 21–23). Saul does not realize that he has invited his replacement into the palace.

The small detail of Saul's servant knowing about David's skill with the harp, which leads to David being invited to Saul's court, is one more example of how the Lord works through various means to bring about his sovereign purposes.

Thus begins David's story. He is to become one of the most prominent characters in biblical history, being the main subject of the rest of 1 Samuel and all of 2 Samuel, along with much of 1 Chronicles. He is the composer of dozens of psalms and is referred to over fifty times in the New Testament. We will see him as a shepherd, a musician, a giant-slayer, a loyal friend, a lover, a warrior, a father, a worshiper, and a king.

Where do we see Jesus in this passage?

When David enters the picture, the allusions to Jesus, the son of David (Matt. 1:1; Rom. 1:3) multiply. Just as David was the king chosen by God (16:1), so God said of Jesus, "This is My Son, My chosen One" (Luke 9:35). Just as Samuel was eager to see David (16:11), so a few faithful saints eagerly awaited the revelation of the Messiah (Luke 2:29–32). Jesus, like David, was born in Bethlehem (1 Sam. 16:1; Micah 5:2; Matt. 2:6). Jesus, again like David, was not chosen according to his outward appearance (1 Sam. 16:7): "He has no stately form or majesty that we should look upon Him, nor appearance that we should be attracted to Him" (Isa. 53:2). Jesus, like David, lived in obscurity before beginning his glorious public work (Luke 2:40; Heb. 5:8). Like David, Jesus had to patiently endure obscurity and suffering before entering into his glory as King. Jesus surpasses David as the Shepherd King who faithfully tends his sheep (John 10:11).

How does this passage apply to us?

- We, like Samuel, can be guilty of judging others based upon outward appearance (v. 7a). We tend to be impressed by outward beauty, clothes, academic success, and wealth, none of which is important to God. James warns us not to show favoritism in the church based upon worldly considerations such as wealth: "My brethren, do not hold your faith in our glorious Lord Jesus Christ with an attitude of personal favoritism" (James 2:1). This also applies to how we choose our friends, how a single person looks for a mate (Prov. 31:30; Ruth 3:11), and how we look for a church home.

- We should be careful not to choose our church leaders according to worldly considerations. Some churches seek pastors who are good-looking, eloquent, and humorous. They also seek lay leaders who have been successful in their careers. Yet God describes the leaders for whom he is looking in terms of their characters and godliness (1 Tim. 3:1–13). More important than the kind of car a man drives or the size of house he owns is the quality of his relationship with his wife and children. More important than his ability to dazzle people with his sermons is whether he is a humble man of prayer who can control his self-will and anger and submit to the Lord and his fellow leaders. We need leaders who will, like David and his greater son, Jesus, shepherd the flock of God (Acts 20:28).
- The Lord continues to make surprising choices, like that of David, which are contrary to worldly considerations. "For consider your calling, brethren, that there were not many wise according to the flesh, not many mighty, not many noble; but God has chosen the foolish things of the world to shame the wise, and God has chosen the weak things of the world to shame the things which are strong, and the base things of the world and the despised God has chosen, the things that are not, so that He may nullify the things that are, so that no man may boast before God" (1 Cor. 1:26–29).
- The fact that God sees beyond our outward appearance into our hearts (16:7) is sobering. What does God see when

he looks at you? Does he see someone who, like Saul, is only concerned about what other people see (15:24)? Or does he see within you, like David, a heart for God? None of us is good by nature, but God offers forgiveness and gives new hearts to all who turn to him in repentance and faith (Ezek. 36:25–26).

- God's rejection of Saul as king and the torment which Saul endured should remind us of the terrible consequences of disobeying the Lord. The fleshly, self-centered life is a hard life. God often punishes sinners by giving them over to more sin (Rom. 1:24, 26, 28).

FOR FURTHER STUDY

1. Did the Lord tell Samuel to mislead Saul by saying that he was going to Bethlehem to offer sacrifice (16:2; 15:29; also see Exod. 5:1)?
2. Are we ever justified in deceiving others? Is it permissible to conceal the truth from those who have no right to it?
3. In what sense did the Holy Spirit come upon David (16:13)? Does the Spirit indwell believers today in the same or a different way?
4. How could the Spirit depart from Saul (16:14)? Can a true believer lose the Holy Spirit (see Eph. 1:13–14; Phil. 1:6)?
5. What power does God have over evil spirits (16:15; Judg. 9:23; 1 Kings 22:20–23; 1 Chr. 21:1; 2 Sam. 24:1; Job 2:10; 1 Cor. 5:5; 2 Cor. 12:7–10)?

TO THINK ABOUT AND DISCUSS

1. When are we tempted to judge others according to their outward appearance?
2. What criteria should we use to select our leaders? Our friends?
3. What consequences might we experience when we disobey God?
4. Does music have spiritual uses and effects today (16:23)? See Colossians 3:16 and Ephesians 5:19–20.
5. How does this passage point to Christ?

9 David defeats Goliath

(17:1–58)

The account of David and Goliath is one of the most famous in all literature. This is a tale of might versus right in which the little guy beats up the bully. This story is part of our common culture. When the underdog wins a sporting event or an election, we say that David has defeated Goliath.

Sadly, many have misunderstood the significance of David's encounter with Goliath. For example, there is a children's VeggieTales video, *Dave and the Giant Pickle*, in which "Dave, upset over not being allowed to join his brothers who have all gone off to war, is resigned to staying at home and taking care of the farm. When a giant pickle is sent to attack his village, Dave relies on God's teachings, and his own self-esteem, to fight the monster."[1] Yet this story is not primarily about David, but about the Lord whom David represents. With whom are we primarily to identify in this account? We are not by nature like David, who bravely conquers his enemy. Rather, we are like the fearful people who desperately need a champion to defeat an enemy they are incapable of facing.

The big picture

The encounter between David and Goliath is part of the cosmic battle which began in Genesis 3, when Satan defeated Adam and gained dominion over the earth (1 John 5:19). At that time the Lord promised that a champion would come, born of a woman, who would crush the serpent/Satan (Gen. 3:15). God later chose the family of Abraham, to whom he gave a great land and people, to be the nation through which he would bring deliverance to humanity. As we come to 1 Samuel 17, Abraham's people are unable to enjoy their land because they are being harassed by their idolatrous enemies, the Philistines, who are represented by the blaspheming, arrogant Goliath. Israel needs a champion to deliver her from the Satanic oppressor. The people's king, Saul, proves to be unworthy, so the Lord raises up a new champion, David, who defeats Israel's enemies through God's strength, thus delivering the people. David's victory points ahead to Jesus, the son of David, who will win the ultimate victory over Satan, thus securing everlasting deliverance for the people of God, Abraham's children (Gal. 3:7).

Goliath defies and terrorizes Israel (vv. 1–11)

Israel and the Philistines have reached a kind of military stalemate as both sides have dug in (vv. 1–3). Goliath, the champion of the Philistines, challenges Israel to send forth a man to fight him in representative combat. Those represented by the loser will surrender to the winner (vv. 8–10). Goliath is a massive human fighting machine, over nine feet tall, heavily armored, and armed (vv. 4–6). Goliath is much worse than a big bully. He is a blasphemer who curses the Lord and his people (vv. 10, 16, 26, 36, 45). The same Hebrew word used of Goliath taking his stand in verse 16 is used in Psalm 2 of the kings of the earth who take their stand against the Lord and his Anointed One (Ps. 2:2), making Goliath an antichrist figure. Goliath should worship Israel's God and submit to Israel's anointed king. Instead, he arrogantly defies them. Such defiance of God invites his judgment (Ps. 2:4–12).

Saul and his army are overwhelmed by fear of Goliath (vv. 11, 24) and refuse to take up his challenge. They should trust God, who stands with his people who oppose mighty oppressors (which is a theme of Hannah's song, 2:3–4, 9–10). "The LORD is the one who goes ahead of you; He will be with you. He will not fail you or forsake you. Do not fear or be dismayed" (Deut. 31:8; also see 20:1–4). Saul, as the king who has been appointed to fight the people's battles (8:20; 9:16), should go forth in faith. Instead, he hangs back in fear and unbelief, offering a reward to anyone who will fight his battle for him (17:25). The fear of Israel is, like that of the ten spies in Moses' day (Num. 13:32–33), due to unbelief. The Israelites see as man sees, rather than as God sees (1 Sam. 16:7). As a result, they endure forty days of terror (17:16).

David steps forward to accept Goliath's challenge (vv. 12–40)

David is not with Saul's army to hear Goliath's initial challenge, probably because he is too young for military service. David is sent by his father, Jesse, to check on his older brothers and to bring them food (vv. 12–19). Little does Jesse imagine what he is sending David to do. When David arrives on the battlefield he gets a close-up view of Goliath and the fearful Israelite troops (vv. 20–25). David, in his first recorded words, eloquently expresses indignation over the blasphemy of Goliath, the uncircumcised pagan who taunts the armies of the living God (v. 26; circumcision was the sign of God's covenant with his people). Incidentally, David uses the same language Jonathan used when he bravely attacked the Philistine garrison (14:6), showing that these were men of like hearts and faith. David is a man who sees as God sees and is zealous for the Lord's honor (Ps. 69:9). David's fleshly brother Eliab misunderstands David's motives and wrongly rebukes him (17:27–30).

When Saul hears that there is a man who is brave enough to fight Goliath, he sends for David (vv. 31–32). Saul, who sees only with the eyes of the flesh, doubts whether David can prevail (v. 33). David, recalling how the Lord has delivered him in the past from the lion and the bear, expresses full confidence that the Lord will deliver him again (vv. 34–37a). David's faith enables him to see how big God is and how small that makes Goliath. Like Jonathan (14:6), David is not afraid to go against seemingly impossible odds, knowing that the Lord is with him. His trust is not in his own bravery, skill, or self-esteem, but in the Lord. Saul finally agrees and wishes David well (v. 37b). David refuses Saul's armor because he is not accustomed to it, and instead prepares his own sling and stones for battle (vv. 38–40).

The combatants make their taunt speeches (vv. 41–47)

David goes alone to the field of combat, where Goliath immediately approaches him. Before battle each man taunts the other. Goliath, full of self-confidence, curses David and, by implication, the Lord whom David represents (vv. 41–44). "The kings of the earth take their stand and the rulers take counsel together against the LORD and against His Anointed" (Ps. 2:2). This is not merely a contest between two men; it is cosmic combat between the gods of the Philistines and the Lord God of Israel.

What should Goliath have done?

> Now therefore, O kings, show discernment;
> Take warning, O judges of the earth.
> Worship the LORD with reverence
> And rejoice with trembling.
> Do homage to the Son, that He not become angry, and you perish in the way,
> For his wrath may soon be kindled.
>
> (Ps. 2:10–12)

Goliath should have bowed down before David, the anointed one of the only God. Instead, Goliath's arrogance invites God's holy wrath, for God is "opposed to the proud" (James 4:6). "You [God] shall break them with a rod of iron, you shall shatter them like earthenware" (Ps. 2:9).

> Goliath's arrogance invites God's holy wrath, for God is "opposed to the proud" (James 4:6).

David also speaks boldly, with full confidence in the Lord. He clearly defines what is at stake.

"You come to me with a sword, a spear, and a javelin, but I come to you in the name of the LORD of hosts, the God of the armies of Israel, whom you have taunted" (v. 45). David knows that he is an instrument of God's judgment against an antichrist and he expresses certainty that the Lord will give him victory (v. 46). David intends this battle to be a lesson to those fearful, unbelieving men in Israel: "that all this assembly may know that the LORD does not deliver by sword or by spear; for the battle is the LORD's and He will give you into our hands" (v. 47).

The combat and its aftermath (vv. 48–58)

After such a long buildup, the warfare takes place quickly. David boldly runs out to meet Goliath and fells him with a stone hurled from his sling (vv. 48–49). "When evildoers came upon me to devour my flesh, my adversaries and my enemies, they stumbled and fell" (Ps. 27:2). David then beheads Goliath with his own sword (vv. 50–51a). Goliath becomes like his false god Dagon, who was decapitated when the ark of the covenant was taken into the Philistine temple (5:1–5). "Those who make them [idols] will become like them, everyone who trusts in them" (Ps. 115:8). False gods and those who worship them cannot stand before the Lord.

After Goliath's death, the Philistines flee and the Israelites take courage and strike down many of their enemies (vv. 51b–54). Saul again takes notice of David, no doubt planning to make further use of his abilities (vv. 55–58). The outcome will be the continued rise of David in Israel. After Saul's pitiful failures, finally God has raised up a man who can deliver Israel from her enemies.

Where do we see Jesus in this passage?

This passage is not primarily about how we can overcome our big problems in life with God's help or how to deal with bullies. We are not to primarily identify with David; rather, we are like the army of Israel, which faces a terrifying enemy which it cannot defeat. We, like the Israelites, need a great champion, anointed by God, to fight our battle and gain the victory we could never achieve. Jesus is the Champion whom God promised would crush Satan (Gen. 3:15). Just as David won the victory over Goliath without the help of Israel's fearful army, so Jesus Christ went to the cross alone and defeated Satan, sin, and death for us.

Like David, Jesus was zealous for the Lord's honor in the face of blasphemy (John 2:14–17; Ps. 69:9). Just as David was rejected by his brothers (17:28), so Jesus was rejected by his (John 1:11; 7:5). Just as David bravely entered into battle against Goliath (17:48), so Jesus boldly set his face to go to the cross for us (Luke 9:51). Jesus also faced blasphemous, arrogant foes who thought that they could destroy him (Matt. 26:4; John 11:53). Just as Goliath was defeated by David, thus setting the people of Israel free from the terror of slavery to the Philistines, so Satan has been conquered by Jesus, our Anointed Champion, setting us free. "Since the children share in flesh and blood, He Himself likewise also partook of the same, that through death He might render powerless him who had the power of death, that is, the devil, and might free those who through fear of death were subject to slavery all their lives" (Heb. 2:14–15; also see 1 John 3:8; Col. 2:13–15; Luke 10:17–18).

How does this passage apply to us?

- In light of the fact that Jesus, like David, has singlehandedly defeated our enemy, we, like the people of Israel, can follow him and participate in his victory. Because of the victory Christ has won for us, we can strive to imitate David. We, too, should be passionate for God's honor. We are set free from the fear of man to serve God (Prov. 29:25). Like David, we can strengthen our faith by recalling God's past faithfulness (1 Sam. 17:35–36), especially in the great deliverance wrought by Christ (Rom. 8:31–39).
- We must also be careful not to fight God's battles in Saul's armor. Some churches today are tempted to rely upon unbiblical methodologies of marketing and psychology rather than the simplicity of the gospel, which to the world may be foolishness but to us is the power of God (1 Cor. 1:18; Heb. 4:12).
- We still have battles to fight against the world, the flesh, and the devil. We war against our own remaining sin. We seek to bring the gospel to enemy strongholds. We defend the truth of God's Word against error (2 Cor. 10:3–5). Because Christ is our Champion, we dare attempt great things for God in missions and evangelism. We can even resist the devil (James 4:7).
- Again we see that the fact that God is with us does not negate human strategy and effort. David prepared for battle by bringing his sling and his stones. He ran toward Goliath to gain

> The fact that God is with us does not negate human strategy and effort.

momentum so he could sling the stone as hard as possible. He aimed the stone at Goliath's head. God achieves his victories through the use of legitimate means, including our trying our best. "For it is for this we labor and strive, because we have fixed our hope on the living God" (1 Tim. 4:10). We should worship, serve, and evangelize with all our hearts and with all our abilities. We also learn from David that the bold faith of a few can inspire the many (17:52–53). We also must, with David, remember that God alone receives the glory for our victory.

FOR FURTHER STUDY

1. What other cosmic battles take place in Scripture?
2. Study Psalm 2 and observe how it parallels this passage.
3. How does this passage illustrate the principle that God wins the victory but we are also responsible for using wise strategies and exerting effort?

TO THINK ABOUT AND DISCUSS

1. Who should have fought Goliath? Why didn't he?
2. Why was David fearless? How can we imitate his faith?
3. With whom should we most identify in this passage? Why?
4. Where in this passage can we see Christ?

10 David and Jonathan

(18:1–20:42)

Each of us needs friends. Friendship has taken on new meaning as people now connect with one another over the Internet, using social-networking sites such as Facebook. Some boast of having hundreds or even thousands of "friends." Yet such "friendships" are very shallow compared with the biblical standard of loyal, loving friendship as described in the book of Proverbs.

The most famous Old Testament example of friendship is that between David and Jonathan, the son of Saul. Their friendship displays many of the characteristics of wise friendships described in Proverbs.

David prospers and is (almost) universally loved (18:5–30; 19:8–24)

After his great victory over Goliath, David continues to enjoy great success in all that he does, because the Lord is with him (18:5, 14, 30). Everyone in Israel loves David (18:16), including Saul's daughter, Michal, who is given in marriage to David as a reward for slaying many Philistines (18:20–29).

However, King Saul, who once also loved David (16:21), becomes insanely jealous and fearful when he hears the people praising David (18:6–9, 15, 29). He becomes determined to kill David, even using his own daughters as pawns in his schemes (18:10–11, 17, 25; 19:8–10). David needs a friend to keep him safe from Saul. The Lord supplies just such a friend from Saul's own household.

Jonathan befriends David (18:1–4; 19:1–7; 20:1–42)

"The soul of Jonathan was knit to the soul of David, and Jonathan loved him as himself" (18:1). This is, in one sense, an unlikely friendship. Jonathan is the crown prince and the heir apparent to the throne. David, who is doing kingly work in fighting the Philistines and has the affection of the people, could be seen by Jonathan as a rival. On the other hand, David and Jonathan have much in common as men of like faith, zeal, and courage. Both fought the Philistines when the odds were against them and while others, including King Saul, were afraid. Both boldly attacked Israel's enemies because they trusted in the Lord (13:3; 14:6–15; 17:26, 36, 47). This common faith and zeal for the Lord knits their souls together (18:1). The same language is used of Jacob: his soul was knit to the life of his youngest son, Benjamin (Gen. 44:30). Jonathan loves David as himself. While some modern commentators have tried to use this passage along with others (2 Sam. 1:26) to claim that there was a romantic or sexual relationship between David and Jonathan, this is a love of friendship as commanded in God's law (Lev. 19:18), not romance. Indeed, the word for love used here is used of others who loved David, including Saul (16:21) and all Israel (18:16). The theme of this section is that everyone loves David. Both David and Jonathan are godly married men who keep God's law, which forbids homosexual activity (Lev. 20:13). Their love for each other is demonstrated by their actively doing good for each other. "Little children, let us not love with word or with tongue, but in deed and truth" (1 John 3:18).

Jonathan and David make a covenant as an expression of their commitment to each other (18:3). Jonathan, as the man of higher rank, takes the initiative (Jonathan was probably older than David as he had already been serving in the military when David was still too young to fight). We are not told the specific content of their agreement, but subsequent events make it clear that they promise to be loyal to each other through thick and thin. As a result, Jonathan defends David against Saul's false accusations (19:1–7) and warns David about Saul's plot to murder him (20:1–42). Jonathan pays a price for his faithfulness to David, as his deranged father becomes enraged against Jonathan and even seeks to kill him (20:30–34; 22:6–8). Later, when David is hiding from Saul in the wilderness, Jonathan encourages him in God, saying, "Do not be afraid, because the hand of Saul my father will not find you, and you will be king over Israel and I will be next to you" (23:17). Then, after Saul and Jonathan are dead, David fulfills his covenant promise (20:15, 42) by caring for Jonathan's son, Mephibosheth (2 Sam. 9:1–13). This act of David's stands out in the ancient world, when the normal practice was to exterminate the descendants of the old dynasty, lest they become rivals.

Jonathan signifies the sealing of their covenant by giving David his royal robe and armor (18:4). In ancient times, clothing denoted status; for example, Joseph's coat of many colors signified that he was chief among his brothers (Gen. 37:3). Later, when Joseph was elevated to prime minister of Egypt, he exchanged his lowly prisoner's garments for clothing befitting his new status (Gen. 41:41–42). Likewise, when Aaron died, his priestly garments were given to his son, Eleazar (Num. 20:23–28). It appears that Jonathan is relinquishing his status as crown prince to David. In so doing, it seems that Jonathan is aware that David has been chosen and anointed by God as the next king (16:1, 13; 23:17).

Where do we see Jesus in this passage?

Jonathan's willingness to give up his status to David, the anointed one, reminds us of John the Baptist, who gladly humbled himself before Jesus the Christ. When John's disciples became jealous of Jesus, John replied,

> You yourselves are my witnesses that I said, "I am not the Christ," but, "I have been sent ahead of Him." He who has the bride is the bridegroom; but the friend of the bridegroom, who stands and hears him, rejoices greatly because of the bridegroom's voice. So this joy of mine has been made full. He must increase, but I must decrease.
>
> (John 3:28–30)

John, like Jonathan, was not jealous of the Lord's Anointed, but was glad that he would receive the kingdom God had given him. Again like Jonathan, John died before he could see the kingdom come to fruition (1 Sam. 31:2; Mark 6:27).

Just as Jonathan's loyalty to David brought division from his father Saul, so loyalty to Jesus brings division within families (Matt. 10:34–36). In contrast to Goliath and Saul, who opposed David (see Ps. 2:2–3), resulting in their destruction (Ps. 2:4–6, 9), Jonathan humbled himself before the Lord's anointed (1 Sam. 18:4; also see Ps. 2:10–12). So all should humble themselves before the Lord Jesus Christ, before whom every knee will one day bow (Phil. 2:9–11).

Your human friendships often fall short because people let you down (Jer. 17:5–6). Jesus, however, is the friend of sinners who will never disappoint you (Luke 7:34; Jer. 17:7–8). He perfectly exemplifies all that Scripture teaches about friendship. He loves you at all times (Prov. 17:17) with an everlasting covenant love from before the foundation of the world. He loves you, even while knowing how sinful you are. His love will endure forever. Just as Jonathan risked his life to rescue David, so Jesus laid down his life to show his love to you. "Greater love has no one than this, that one lay down his life for his friends" (John 15:13).

Just as Jonathan invited David into a covenant friendship, so Jesus invites you to become his friend by grace through faith in him. As his friend, you show your love for him by doing his will: "You are My friends if you do what I command you" (John 15:14). What a privilege it is to be a friend of Jesus (John 15:15)!

The covenant faithfulness of David and Jonathan is a reminder of God's covenant faithfulness to us, supremely expressed in the work of Jesus Christ.

How does this passage apply to us?

- Unlike Saul, who was jealous and angry because of David's success, we should be like Jonathan and rejoice when God sees fit to use others in great ways, even when they surpass us.
- God has made us social beings. Like David, we all need friends (Eccles. 4:9–12). Christ has designed his church to be a community of the mutually dependent, in which none can thrive in isolation (1 Cor. 12). It is foolish to separate yourself from others (Prov. 18:1).
- Just as David and Jonathan's friendship was built upon their mutual faithfulness to God, we are told to choose our friends wisely because our friends will have a powerful influence on us. "He who walks with wise men will be wise, but the companion of fools will suffer harm" (Prov. 13:20). Foolish friends, including those who are hot-tempered, gluttons, drunkards, or slanderers, will ruin you (Prov. 14:7; 22:24–25; 16:29; 23:20; 20:19; 1 Cor. 15:33). Some seek friendship for the wrong reasons: "Wealth adds many friends … Many will seek the favor of a generous man, and every man is a friend to him who gives gifts" (Prov. 19:4a, 6). Parents should take special interest in the friends their children make because young people can be attracted to the wrong kinds of companions (Prov. 1:10–19).

> We are told to choose our friends wisely because our friends will have a powerful influence on us.

- While you may have hundreds of acquaintances (or Facebook friends), you can have only a few close friends. "A man of too many friends comes to ruin, but there is a friend who sticks closer than a brother" (Prov. 18:24). In his earthly ministry, Jesus had a limited number of close friends, the twelve. True friends are rare and should be treasured (Prov. 20:6).
- Just as David and Jonathan proved their love by their actions, so friendship requires effort. Friendship can be ruined through gossip, quarrels, and faithlessness (Prov. 17:9; 16:28; 25:19). Friendship can be cultivated by being trustworthy and loyal, even in hardship. "A friend loves at all times, and a brother is born for adversity" (Prov. 17:17; also see 27:10; 11:13).
- Just as Jonathan and David kept their covenant obligations to each other, so we are reminded that we should keep our commitments to our friends, families, and churches.
- Because we all sin, friendship requires patience and forgiveness (Prov. 17:9; 19:11). Just as Jonathan encouraged David (23:15–16), so friends offer one another wise counsel and encouragement (Prov. 27:9). Friends also show their love by offering needed correction. "Better is open rebuke than love that is concealed. Faithful are the wounds of a friend, but deceitful are the kisses of an enemy" (Prov. 27:5–6). A true friend will make you a better person: "Iron sharpens iron, so one man sharpens another" (Prov. 27:17).

FOR FURTHER STUDY

1. Are there times when adult children may rightly take a stand against their parents, just as Jonathan chose loyalty to his friend, David, over his father, King Saul? How might this have applied to adult children whose parents chose to follow the ten unbelieving spies in Numbers 13–14?
2. What other examples of godly friendship can be found in Scripture?
3. How is Jonathan's response to David, the Lord's anointed, reflected in other places in Scripture? See, for example, Psalm 2 and John 3:25–30.

TO THINK ABOUT AND DISCUSS

1. What are the benefits of having close friends?
2. What kinds of friends do you seek? Why?
3. It has been observed that men today have a hard time forming close friendships. Why might this be? Does our culture's promotion of homosexuality make some men fearful of being intimate friends with other men? What can be done to help godly men form closer friendships?
4. What are the possible benefits and dangers of "friendships" on social networking sites like Facebook?
5. How much time do people need to spend together to maintain a friendship?
6. How is Jesus the perfect friend?
7. How can a person be friends with Jesus?

11 Man on the run

(21:1–24:22; 26:1–25)

Many years ago there was a popular television show called *The Fugitive*, which featured a doctor who, wrongly convicted of his wife's murder, escaped from custody and was constantly on the move, trying to avoid the police. The final third of 1 Samuel portrays David as an innocent fugitive evading King Saul, who, in his jealousy, treats David as a traitor and seeks to kill him. These stories further reveal David's godly character, Saul's vile nature, and the Lord's faithfulness in repeatedly delivering his anointed one.

David's great escapes

While David was still part of Saul's court he repeatedly managed to evade Saul's spear (18:10–11; 19:10) and to escape Saul's plots to kill him through battle with the Philistines (18:17–29), in his own home (19:11–24), and at the royal table (20:31–34). Furthermore, in spite of Saul's efforts to destroy him, David continued to prosper (18:29–30).

Now, David finally leaves Saul and spends years hiding in the wilderness, where he gathers a band of renegades to fight alongside him (22:1–2). While David is on the run the Lord provides for him at Nob (21:1–9), protects him when he hides among the Philistines (21:11–15), guides him through prophets and priests (22:1–5; 23:2, 6–12), and repeatedly helps him to evade Saul (23:13–29). At one point, Saul and his army are on one side of a mountain, with David on the other (23:26). Just as Saul is moving in for the kill, a providential message arrives, which forces Saul to depart to defend the land from the Philistines (23:27).

David's godly character

Many of David's psalms are believed to have been written during his time on the run; in them he bemoans his mistreatment and cries out to God for deliverance (e.g. Ps. 56:1). David decries the arrogance of evil men like Doeg and Saul, who do evil (Ps. 52:1–4). David also expresses praise to the Lord for repeatedly rescuing him (Ps. 34:1) and hopes that the wicked will be destroyed in the end (Ps. 52:5–7).

In his exile, David seeks and submits to the Lord's guidance (22:5; 23:1–13) and continues to fight the enemies of God's people (23:1–5).

On two occasions, David has an opportunity to kill Saul (24:1–22; 26:1–25), but each time he refuses to take his own revenge because Saul has been anointed by God (26:9). David will not seize the kingdom by force, but trusts God to vindicate and enthrone him in due time.

Saul's godless duplicity

Though Saul knows that David has been chosen by God (23:17), he relentlessly persists in trying to murder him. Saul wickedly puts to death the innocent priests who helped David at Nob (22:6–23). When David twice spares his life, Saul appears to humble himself, admitting that David is in the right and promising to stop seeking to kill him (24:16–22; 26:21–27): "I have sinned. Return, my son David, for I will not harm you again because my life was precious in your sight this day. Behold, I have played the fool" (26:21). Both times, however, Saul goes back on his word and renews his murderous pursuit of David. Saul's culpability is all the greater in light of the fact that he admits that David is the rightful future king, anointed by God: "Now, behold, I know that you will surely be king" (24:20; also see 26:25). Because the Lord is with David and has departed from Saul, the king's wicked efforts are in vain, in spite of his military advantage. The time of Saul's demise and David's elevation draws near.

Where do we see Jesus in this passage?

David, in his experience of suffering before entering into his glory, is a type of Jesus, the Son of David, who also endured rejection and suffering before he entered into his glory. The disciples (and the Jews who had the Old Testament) should not have been surprised by this (Luke 24:25–27). The psalms in which David reflected upon his troubles and looked to God's deliverance were fulfilled in Christ's life and death. "He keeps all his bones, not one of them is broken" (Ps. 34:20; John 19:33, 36).

Though Jesus, like David, had done much good (1 Sam. 19:4; John 19:4, 6; Luke 23:47), those in authority, like Saul, sought to destroy him because of jealousy (Luke 20:19; Acts 4:27). Because of God's protection, their attempts to harm Jesus, like Saul's attempts to kill David, were repeatedly thwarted (John 7:30; 8:59). Even after his enemies succeeded in killing Jesus, God delivered him from the grave (Acts 2:23–36) and exalted his Anointed One.

Just as David did not revenge himself on Saul, so Jesus did not retaliate against those who hated and reviled him, but entrusted himself to God (1 Peter 2:23).

Just as David refused to prematurely take his crown by killing Saul, so Jesus refused the many temptations he faced to seize his kingdom prematurely (Matt. 4:1–11; Mark 8:31–33). Jesus, like David, was absolutely determined to submit to God's plan as to the timing and the means by which his glorious kingdom would be gained.

Just as David won his bride, Michal, by destroying the enemies of God's people (18:17–29), so Jesus won his bride by conquering our great enemy (Gen. 3:15; Col. 2:15; Rom. 16:20).

Just as David cared for his family in a time of distress (22:3), so Jesus made sure that his mother Mary was cared for (John 19:26–27).

Jesus, like David at Keilah, was betrayed by those for whom he had done great good (1 Sam. 23:1–12; Ps. 41:9; John 10:31–32).

Just as the people of God sang of David's triumphs (1 Sam. 18:6–7), so God's people joyously sing of Jesus's great victory (Rev. 5:12–14; Ps. 59:16–17).

Just as David surrounded himself with outcasts (1 Sam. 22:2), so Jesus surrounds himself with sinners, welcoming those whom the world rejects and allowing them the privilege of sharing in his coming kingdom (Matt. 9:10–13; 1 Cor. 1:26–31).

Just as even Saul begrudgingly acknowledged David to be the rightful king (24:19–20), so one day even Jesus's enemies will acknowledge his Lordship (Phil. 2:9–11).

Just as David was the rightful king living in exile, so, in our age, Jesus is the rightful King who has yet to be enthroned over the earth. We eagerly wait for that day (Rev. 22:20).

How does this passage apply to us?

- The experiences of David and Jesus reflect the ongoing experiences of God's people. We, too, will be oppressed by the world, which hates and envies us because of our connection to Christ (John 15:18–20). "Do not be surprised, brethren, if the world hates you" (1 John 3:13). Persecution has continued throughout the history of the church. Sadly, many in our day are unprepared for suffering because they have been misled by the false teaching that our best life is now and if we have enough faith we will not suffer in this life. Like David and Jesus, however, our cross will come before our crown. Our best

Sadly, many in our day are unprepared for suffering because they have been misled by the false teaching that our best life is now and if we have enough faith we will not suffer in this life.

life is the life to come, when the travails of this life will be over (Rom. 8:18).

- Like David and Jesus, we may face betrayal from those to whom we have shown love (1 Sam. 23:12, 19; 2 Tim. 4:16; John 16:2).
- Like David, we can trust the Lord to protect and deliver us, even when all the power seems to be on the other side (Ps. 59:8–10). This does not mean that we will not suffer, but that, in the end, we will be vindicated. "Many are the afflictions of the righteous, but the LORD delivers him out of them all" (Ps. 34:19). Those who are in Christ are protected from death and hell.
- We also learn from David's wanderings that God uses means in delivering us. The Lord delivered David, but David had to run and sometimes hide.
- Just as David refused to take revenge on Saul, so Scripture reminds us that it is not our place to take revenge because vengeance belongs to the Lord (Rom. 12:17–21). We are to love our enemies (Matt. 5:43–48).
- Just as David respected King Saul, so we are to respect those God has placed in authority over us—in the government, the home, the workplace, and in the church—even if they are not always worthy of honor (Rom. 13:1–7; Eph. 5:22–33; Heb. 13:17).
- There are also negative applications to be learned from the bad example of Saul, who, in his hateful jealousy, portrays the natural man who is enslaved to sin (John 8:34, 44; Rom. 6:20; Prov. 25:28). Saul is like contemporary tyrants who violate justice and even wage war against their own people in order to maintain their own power.

- Though wicked tyrants and their followers may seem to get away with their atrocities, just as Saul ruthlessly murdered the priests (22:16–19), the Lord will ultimately bring justice.
- Unbelievers may, like Saul, have a conscience and an awareness of truth (1 Sam. 19:6; 24:16–22; 26:21–27), but they cannot live by what they know to be true because they do not have the Spirit of God.
- Saul illustrates the futility and madness of opposing God (Ps. 2:4; 59:8). Will you be like Saul and try to cling to your own authority or glory, seeing Jesus as a threat, or will you submit yourself to the Lord's Anointed? Faith causes and enables us to surrender all our rights and interests to God.

FOR FURTHER STUDY

1. David appeared to mislead the priests at Nob (21:2; also see 19:14). Is deceit ever justified? If so, when? Also see Joshua 2:4 and Exodus 1:15–20.
2. Many people, including the priests at Nob, suffered terribly because of Saul's wicked acts (22:11–19). Why did God allow such terrible evil? See Genesis 50:20; Acts 2:23; and Romans 8:28.
3. How did the Lord's answer to David in 23:10–12 uniquely illustrate God's omniscience? Are there other places in Scripture where God shows that he knows not only what will be, but also what might have been? See, for example, Matthew 11:20–24; 26:24; and 2 Kings 13:19.
4. Some people claim that God leads us by opening doors. Twice David had open doors from God (26:8) to kill Saul, but he refused. How can we know if an open door is God's leading?
5. How can we pray David's psalms when we are oppressed by wickedness (see Ps. 34, 52, 54, 56)?
6. What other examples in the Bible can you find of people who, like Saul, had a conscience and knew something of the truth, but remained hardened?

TO THINK ABOUT AND DISCUSS

1. How was David's experience in these chapters a type of the life of Christ?
2. Why should we expect to suffer in the way that David and Jesus did?
3. David received guidance through prophets and priests. Where do we turn for guidance?
4. What hope can we have when it appears that the forces of evil in the world are much more powerful than we are?

12 David and Abigail

(25:1–44)

During the time that David is on the run from Saul he encounters various temptations. Twice he has the opportunity to kill Saul (chs. 24 and 26), but he resists the opportunity to take revenge. In this chapter, David faces a different temptation to take revenge when he is provoked by a foolish man named Nabal. David is delivered from this temptation through the wise pleadings of Nabal's wife, Abigail. He then sees how God avenges himself against the wicked.

Nabal insults David (vv. 1–13)

As David and his men move through various parts of Israel they provide the local people with protection from their enemies, such as the Philistines or marauding bands of Amalekites (30:1–2). In exchange, David's militia expects some provisions. While Saul views David and his men as traitors and terrorists, we know that David is anointed by God as the rightful future king to whom the people owe respect (Ps. 2:12).

David has now moved to the southern part of Judah, near

Hebron, which is where he encounters Nabal, a man of wealth and importance (v. 2) who is also harsh and evil (v. 3b). Nabal's name actually means "fool" (v. 25). One may wonder what mother would give this name to her son, but it is possible that this was a nickname which was earned later in life. The fact that he is foolish does not mean that he is stupid. Foolishness is a moral, not an intellectual, deficiency. "The fool has said in his heart, 'There is no God.' They are corrupt, they have committed abominable deeds" (Ps. 14:1). Nabal is probably a very shrewd businessman, like many godless titans of commerce today. His foolishness is demonstrated by his proud, careless speech and reckless actions (Prov. 29:11, 20) through which he insults David, the Lord's anointed, thereby putting his family at great risk. Abigail, on the other hand, is a woman of both beauty and wisdom (v. 3a), as we will soon see. Beauty and wisdom are a rare combination in a woman (Prov. 11:22). Interestingly, such qualities are also found in David (16:12). Nabal surely married way above himself; perhaps this mismatch was an arranged marriage.

Foolishness is a moral, not an intellectual, deficiency.

When David hears that Nabal is shearing his sheep (v. 4), he sends a delegation to Nabal to request provisions for his six hundred men, because sheep shearing is a festive time during which the wealthy hold feasts and share with their neighbors (v. 36). David's representatives go through the typical Middle Eastern formalities of offering Nabal a greeting of peace (vv. 5–6), and then they remind him of the benefits of protection he has received from David (v. 7;

also see vv. 15–16). Both the Middle Eastern expectation of hospitality and reciprocity for David's kindness demand that Nabal offer something to David (v. 8). Nabal's obligation is compounded by the fact that he has received no ordinary visitor. This is the opportunity of a lifetime. These men are representing the Lord's anointed, the future king. One's response to God's anointed determines one's destiny (Ps. 2:10). Nabal should, like Abraham (Gen. 18:1–8; Heb. 13:2), have killed the fatted calf in honor of those sent by the Lord.

Instead, Nabal rudely refuses David's request, accusing David's men of a shakedown (or a sheikdown). He belittles and insults David, whom he should have known was the future king (after all, his wife knows—v. 30). He shows himself to be a harsh man who refuses to return good for the good he has received from David (vv. 9–11). Nabal curses the Lord's anointed, the one to whom he should have paid homage. "Do homage to the Son, that He not become angry, and you perish in the way, for His wrath may soon be kindled" (Ps. 2:12). Even common sense dictates that one doesn't insult a man with an army of six hundred men! Nabal, in his pride and foolish opposition to David, reminds us of King Saul.

When David hears of Nabal's rudeness he prepares to take revenge on Nabal (vv. 12–13). He vows to slaughter Nabal and all his menfolk (vv. 21–22). David's thirst for revenge upon Nabal is a sad contrast to his refusal to avenge himself upon Saul (chs. 24 and 26). His vengeance is also disproportionate, as he seeks to kill many (all the males in Nabal's household) for the sins of one. David sounds like Saul with his proud, violent, impetuous anger. David shows himself to be a sinner who needs deliverance. Thankfully, the Lord sends David a (surprising) deliverer.

Abigail rescues her family from death and David from sin (vv. 14–31)

After Nabal insults David, one of Nabal's servants tells Abigail what has happened (vv. 14–18). This is probably not the first time the servants have gone around their master to his wiser wife. This time their lives are at stake. The servant affirms and expands upon what David's representatives have said about David's men having been good to Nabal's workers (vv. 15–16). Note that, while David's men were "a wall" of protection to Nabal's servants (v. 16), foolish Nabal is like the city with its walls broken down (Prov. 25:28). The servant rightly concludes that David is planning to wipe out Nabal and his house, including the servants. He also realizes that there is no use trying to change Nabal's mind (v. 17).

Abigail springs into action. She is a wise woman who knows just what to do and acts quickly. She prepares a large gift of food which she hopes will propitiate (turn aside the anger of) David, and rushes to meet him (vv. 18–20). She finds David just in time, even as he is on the verge of totally destroying her household (vv. 20–22).

Abigail's appeal to David, which is one of the longest speeches by a woman in Scripture, is a masterpiece of female wisdom and charm (vv. 23–31). Though Abigail is a wealthy noblewoman, she approaches David humbly and respectfully, bowing before the anointed one (vv. 23–24). She takes the guilt of her husband upon herself (v. 24a; this echoes Paul's asking of Philemon to put whatever wrong Onesimus had done to his account—Philem. 1:18), perhaps in light of the fact that in marriage the two are one (Gen. 2:24). Abigail doesn't make excuses for worthless Nabal, but acknowledges that his foolish character fits his name. She asks David to pay attention to her instead of to her husband, stating that she has, until recently, been unaware of the evil that he has done to David's servants (v. 25).

Abigail then wisely points David to the Lord. She gives thanks that God has restrained David from vengefully shedding blood (v. 26a). She pleads with him to receive her gift of provisions as restitution and to forgive her transgression, which came through the act of her husband (vv. 27–28a). She also encourages David by affirming that the Lord will exalt, protect, and avenge him (vv. 28b–29). Though David appears to be in a position of weakness as he is being chased by Saul's army and is regarded by many, including her husband, as a renegade (v. 10), Abigail, like Jonathan (23:17), has faith that David will one day reign over all Israel and that his dynasty will last forever. She warns David that, if he takes revenge now, he will one day regret tainting his kingdom in this way; but David can trust the Lord to avenge him against his enemies in due time (vv. 30–31). Vengeance belongs to the Lord (Deut. 32:35).

David heeds Abigail's wise words (vv. 32–35)

Unlike Nabal (v. 17), David is willing to listen to wise counsel, even from a woman. He praises the Lord for sending Abigail to him to keep him from vengeful bloodshed (vv. 32–34). David accepts her propitiatory offering, grants forgiveness, and sends her away in peace (v. 35). What a woman!

A funeral and a wedding (vv. 36–44)

Nabal, in ignorance of his wife's activities which have saved his life, holds a great feast, showing that he has plenty of resources with which he could have blessed David instead of cursing him. The next morning, after Nabal is recovering from his hangover from the previous night's festivities, Abigail tells him what she did to turn away David's wrath. When Nabal hears the news, his heart fails him. So that there will be no question as to why this happened, we are told, "The LORD struck Nabal and he died" (v. 38). Abigail's expectation of the Lord's judgment upon David's enemies (v. 29) is fulfilled immediately in the death of Nabal and will soon be realized in the death of Saul (31:1–6).

Nabal's loss becomes David's gain. When David hears that Nabal has died, he gives thanks to the Lord for keeping him from sinful vengeance and for his justice (v. 39a). David sends a proposal asking Abigail, who is now free (1 Cor. 7:39), to be his wife. Abigail humbly and quickly accepts. She is willing to be a wandering fugitive with David, knowing that one day he will be king (vv. 39b–42).

However, we are told that David had other wives (vv. 43–44). This is contrary to God's design that the two be one flesh (Gen. 2:24; Matt. 19:5) and his command that kings not multiply wives (Deut. 17:17). The Lord tolerated polygamy during Old Testament times, but it always created problems. David's weakness for women would later cause him and the nation a great deal of trouble (2 Sam. 11–12).

The hero of 1 Samuel 25 is not David or even Abigail, but the Lord, who restrains David from sinning and brings judgment upon the wicked, working out his perfect, sovereign purposes through his chosen means.

Where do we see Jesus in this passage?

Jesus is the Anointed One who sends his servants offering his peace to all people (1 Sam. 25:5–6; Matt. 10:9–15). When people, like Nabal, reject and insult his servants, they insult and reject Jesus, which will lead to their judgment (1 Sam. 25:29, 38–39). Like David, Jesus did not take personal vengeance on his enemies, but trusted in God's justice (1 Peter 2:21–23).

> When people, like Nabal, reject and insult Jesus's servants, they insult and reject Jesus, which will lead to their judgment.

Abigail's acknowledgment of David as the true anointed of God, even during his time of weakness and suffering, was echoed in that of the dying criminal, who believed that Jesus, though on the cross, would one day have a great kingdom. Just as Abigail asked David to remember her in his kingdom—"When the LORD deals well with my lord, then remember your maidservant" (v. 31b)—so the dying believing criminal said, "Jesus, remember me when You come into Your kingdom!" (Luke 23:42). Just as Abigail was elevated to share in David's kingdom as his wife (vv. 39–42), so the dying criminal was welcomed to share in Jesus's everlasting kingdom: "Truly I say to you, today you shall be with Me in Paradise" (Luke 23:43).

Abigail's actions also find analogy in Jesus's work. Though

Abigail may not be, like David, a type of Christ, her actions are in some ways analogous to the work of Christ. Just as she took the blame of others upon herself (v. 24) and turned aside David's wrath with her offering (vv. 27–28), so Jesus, though innocent, took our blame and propitiated God's wrath against us (1 Peter 3:18; 2 Cor. 5:21; Isa. 5:4–6). Just as Abigail, though she was a person of nobility, was prepared to wash feet (25:41), so the Lord Jesus washed the feet of his disciples (John 13:1–20).

Finally, just as Abigail was invited by David to be his wife (v. 39b), so we are invited to be the bride of Christ through faith in him. And just as Abigail was ready when the bridegroom came (v. 42), so we need to be ready for when Christ, our Bridegroom, comes (Matt. 25:1–10).

How does this passage apply to us?

- We, like David, can be tempted to exact revenge. We too need to be reminded that it is not our place to take our own vengeance, but to trust God to punish the wicked in due time (Rom. 12:17–21).
- Just as David resisted the temptation to take revenge against Saul but nearly avenged himself against Nabal, so we can resist temptation on some occasions while failing in other situations. "Therefore let him who thinks he stands take heed that he does not fall" (1 Cor. 10:12).
- Abigail provides a model of how to wisely appeal to a person in authority. "By forbearance a ruler may be persuaded, and a soft tongue breaks the bone" (Prov. 25:15).
- Abigail is also an example of how to gently confront someone about his or her sin (Gal. 6:1). She approached David

respectfully, seeking permission to be heard (vv. 23–24). She turned David away from his proud, sinful perspective and put his focus back upon the Lord, reminding him of God's character and promises (vv. 26–31).

- Abigail's example also demonstrates that there are occasions when a woman may rightly reprove a man, even if he is not her husband (Matt. 18:15–18; James 5:19–20). (I personally have benefited from such reproofs from godly women in my congregations.)
- The story of Abigail, who was suffering in an unequal marriage, is being repeated today in many families in which one spouse wisely acknowledges God's Anointed while the other spouse foolishly rejects him (1 Peter 3:1; 1 Cor. 7:12–16). The church should have compassion on such men and women.
- Abigail also presents us with some challenges. The Bible teaches women to submit to their husbands and to show them respect (Eph. 5:22–24, 33b). Abigail went behind her husband's back and disregarded his wishes by offering provision to David (vv. 11, 18). She also acknowledged to David that her husband was a fool (v. 25). Abigail rightly determined that it would be wrong for her to do nothing while her family perished. Her duty to God was to rescue her family, even if that involved going against her husband. In rare situations a wife today may, like Abigail, determine that her duty before God to deliver her family from disaster requires her to go against her husband's leadership. For example, if her husband instructs her to lie or to sign a false document, she should refuse. Likewise, his authority does not extend to stopping her from attending church (Heb.

10:25). This principle of obeying God rather than men (Acts 5:29) also applies in other situations in which one is dealing with those in authority (parents, government, church, employer). Ordinarily, a woman who thinks that she is in Abigail's situation should seek counsel from her pastor(s) before taking drastic action.

- Because we are prone to wander, we sometimes need correction. Are you like Nabal, who foolishly refused to listen to others (v. 17; Prov. 15:12, 32a)? Or do you, like David, wisely and gratefully receive counsel and rebuke (vv. 32–35)? "He whose ear listens to the life-giving reproof will dwell among the wise" (Prov. 15:31). Some men, like Nabal, are too proud to receive correction from their wives or others they believe to be inferior to them. Part of a wife's function as a helper to her husband is to lovingly correct him and point him to the Lord (Gen. 2:18; Prov. 31:11–12). Are you, like David, willing to listen to someone who is under your authority or younger than you?
- This passage also illustrates how God delivers us from temptation (Matt. 6:13). When David was on the verge of falling into grave sin, the Lord sent Abigail to admonish him. The Lord also gave David the wisdom to repent from his sin. We should be thankful for God's grace in keeping us from sin and for the people he uses in our lives.
- Nabal is the example of the foolish, proud man who disregards the Lord and his Anointed One. Nabal had no control over his spirit (Prov. 25:28), which made him vulnerable to disaster.
- Like Nabal, you can be rich and successful in an earthly sense and still be a complete fool in the eyes of God.

- We all were once like Nabal, foolish, proud, and independent (Titus 3:3), but God had mercy upon us by forgiving and transforming us, turning our hearts to him (Titus 3:4–8). Because of God's grace we who were once like Nabal can become like Abigail, as we recognize and honor the Lord's Anointed One and enjoy the privileges of being his bride.

FOR FURTHER STUDY

1. David appeared to break his foolish vow to slaughter Nabal's household (vv. 22, 35). Does this imply that other foolish vows may be rightfully repented of (see Judg. 11:30–40; Matt. 14:6–12)?
2. How many of the characteristics of a fool set forth in Proverbs did Nabal exemplify?
3. In what ways does Abigail exhibit the characteristics of a wise woman set forth in Proverbs 31:10–31?

TO THINK ABOUT AND DISCUSS

1. Under what circumstances are you tempted to take revenge upon those who wrong you? How can you overcome this temptation (Rom. 12:17–21)?
2. In what situations may a wife go against her husband's authority?
3. How could Abigail's example be misused by some wives?
4. How can we learn from Abigail how to confront those in authority over us about their sin?
5. What are some of the ways in which we can see Jesus in this passage?

13 The fall of Saul

(27:1–31:13)

Saul was the king for whom the people asked. He was a tall, handsome warrior. He got off to a positive start when he defeated the Ammonites (ch. 11). It wasn't long, however, before Saul proved himself to be unworthy

In his impatience, Saul offered sacrifices before Samuel arrived (13:8–12). Then he failed to fully carry out the Lord's judgment on the Amalekites (15:3, 9). As a result the Lord, through Samuel, declared to Saul, "Your kingdom shall not endure. The LORD has sought out for Himself a man after His own heart, and the LORD has appointed him as ruler over His people, because you have not kept what the LORD commanded you" (13:14; also see 15:23, 26, 28).

The Lord then sent Samuel to anoint David, the man after his own heart who would one day replace Saul as king (ch. 16). David proved himself to be a worthy leader as he, through faith in the Lord, defeated Goliath and continued to fight the Philistines (ch. 17). King Saul, however, became jealous and sought to murder David, pursuing him throughout Israel over many years. With the Lord's help David was repeatedly able to escape. David refused to seize the throne, even when he had the opportunity, but waited on the Lord to remove Saul so that he could reign as king.

Meanwhile, Saul continued to decline personally and spiritually. As we come to the end of 1 Samuel, Saul's end finally comes, not through David, but at the hands of the Philistines. Perhaps Saul's own words are his best epitaph: "I have played the fool" (26:21).

Saul consults a medium (witch) (28:3–25)

Saul is desperate and overwhelmed by fear. He is surrounded by his enemies, the Philistines (vv. 1, 4). He has further weakened himself militarily by driving away David, who is his best general. Worst of all, Saul, in his hour of greatest need, is cut off from the Lord, who refuses to answer him by any of the usual means (v. 6; 16:14). Saul is reaping what he has sown (Gal. 6:7; Amos 8:11–12) by waging war on David, the Lord's anointed, and killing the Lord's priests (22:16–19). The true prophets and priests are with David.

Saul now multiplies his guilt by seeking supernatural guidance through a medium (v. 7). The Lord had forbidden all pagan practices of seeking supernatural power or knowledge apart from through him (Deut. 18:10–14; Lev. 19:31; Isa. 8:19). This further illustrates Saul's decline, because earlier in his reign he had outlawed these practices (v. 9). Now he is acting like a pagan king, inviting the Lord's judgment upon himself (1 Chr. 10:13; note that his earlier disobedience is regarded as wicked as divination—15:23).

Saul asks the medium at En-dor to bring Samuel back from the dead (vv. 8–11). To her own terror she appears to succeed (vv. 12–14).

There is some debate over whether Samuel actually appears. Some contend that what Saul sees is a demonic deception. The text, however, says that it is Samuel, and he certainly speaks as one would expect Samuel to speak (vv. 15–19). This is not the only time that the spirits of dead men visit the living in the Bible (e.g. the transfiguration in Matt. 17:3). The Lord apparently allowed this for his own sovereign purpose. The text of Scripture often does not satisfy our curiosity, but "the secret things belong to the LORD" (Deut. 29:29).

Samuel offers no encouragement or hopeful guidance to Saul. Instead, the prophet declares that Saul's kingdom is being taken away from him because of his stubborn disobedience and will be given to David. Furthermore, Saul and his sons will die the next day at the hands of the Philistines (vv. 15–19). This pronouncement of judgment is almost identical to the judgment Eli received concerning the deaths of his sons and himself in Israel's defeat, and that his line would be replaced by someone better (2:34–35). Now Saul is all the more terrified, to the point of refusing food (vv. 20–25).

Meanwhile, back in Gath … (27:1–28:2; 29:1–30:31)

David, having become weary of being chased by Saul, flees to the Philistines, who receive him because he is estranged from their enemy, Saul (27:1–3). David's plan seems to work, as Saul stops chasing him (27:4). David is given his own city, Ziklag, from which he and his men conduct raids among the enemies of God's people, though untruthfully he tells the Philistines that he has been raiding cities in Israel (27:5–12). David, however, is about to face a grave dilemma, as the Philistines with whom he is living are about to go to war against Saul and they expect him to join them (28:1–2; 29:1–2). Will David fight against Israel? Or will he turn on the Philistines? Through God's gracious providence, this problem is taken out of David's hands when the Philistine commanders send him back to Ziklag because they fear that he will turn on them in battle (29:3–11).

When David and his men return to their temporary home, he faces one of his greatest trials because the Amalekites have raided the defenseless city, burning it with fire and carrying away all the women and children (30:1–3). David and his people are overwhelmed with sorrow (30:4–5). Worst of all, David's men blame him and are speaking of stoning him (30:6a). David turns to the Lord and seeks wisdom through Abiathar, the priest (30:6b–7). While the Lord has refused to answer Saul's inquiry (28:6), he gives direction to David, assuring him that he and his men will be able to rescue the captives (30:8–10). The Lord then gives David a great victory as he catches the Amalekites and wipes them out (30:11–17). He and his men not only regain all that they lost, but they also capture additional spoils (30:18–20). David gives glory to God in victory (30:23) and shows his generosity and wisdom by sharing the spoils equally among his men, even with those who were too exhausted to fight (30:21–25). He also shares his bounty with the people of Judah, who have helped him in the past and whose support he will need in the near future, as the time for him to be enthroned draws near (30:26–31).

The king is dead (31:1–13)

Saul's end comes suddenly. After his sinful séance with the medium at Endor (ch. 28), he leads Israel into battle against the Philistines. Israel's army is crushed and Saul and his sons, sadly including Jonathan, are killed (vv. 1–6). (We will learn that at least one of Saul's sons, Ish-bosheth, survives (2 Sam. 2:8). For a time this son of Saul becomes a rival to David for the throne of Israel.) Saul's death is particularly shameful as he falls on his own sword (v. 4) and his dead body is desecrated by the Philistines, who display it as a sign of the victory of their idols over Israel's God (30:8–10). Like the Assyrians years later, they do not realize that they are merely the rod of God's anger and that they too will be punished in due time (Isa. 10:5–7).

Saul dies a failure, losing his kingdom, his sons, his life, and his dignity. He leaves Israel in a state of disarray, having lost much of the land to Israel's enemies (v. 7). The Philistines are merely the instruments of God's judgment: "So Saul died for his trespass which he committed against the LORD, because of the word of the LORD which he did not keep; and also because he asked counsel of a medium, making inquiry of it, and did not inquire of the LORD. Therefore He killed him and turned the kingdom to David the son of Jesse" (1 Chr. 10:13–14). Saul's death, however, is not the end of the story, but only the end of the first act. The Lord will enthrone a king in Israel who will vindicate his name.

Saul's downfall was foreshadowed in Hannah's song:

Boast no more so very proudly.
Do not let arrogance come out of your mouth;
For the LORD is a God of knowledge,
And with Him actions are weighed.
The bows of the mighty are shattered …
The wicked ones are silenced in darkness.
For not by might shall a man prevail.
Those who contend with the LORD shall be shattered;
Against them He will thunder in the heavens.

(2:3–4a, 9b–10a)

Saul's final defeat stands in sharp contrast to the great victory that David has recently won over the Amalekites. While the Lord is silent when Saul inquires of him (28:6), the Lord hears and helps David (30:7). While the army Saul leads incurs many casualties as it flees from the enemy (31:7), there is no loss of life among David's men, and Israel's enemies are the ones who flee (30:17, 19). The people's failed king is removed in order to make room for God's chosen king to reign over Israel. The Lord, through David, will crush the Philistines, showing that their idols are worthless. David will bring peace and stability to Israel. His story is told in 2 Samuel. Hannah also sang prophetically about David:

The LORD will judge the ends of the earth;
And He will give strength to His king,
And will exalt the horn of His anointed.

(2:10b)

Where do we see Jesus in this passage?

Jesus, like Saul, was forsaken by God, not for his own sin, but for ours (Mark 15:33–34; Isa. 53:4–6). For a short time

God hid his face from Jesus and treated him as an enemy. But because Jesus was forsaken by God, we for whom he died never will be.

Like David, Jesus strengthened himself in God when men rejected him and he pressed on to do God's will (30:6–8; John 11:53). Jesus, like David, is our great leader who won a great victory over God's strong enemy, Satan (30:20; Matt. 12:29). Like David, Jesus rescues all those he came to save, losing none (30:19; John 6:39; 10:29; Isa. 53:11). Like David, Jesus captures spoils which he shares with his people (30:20; Eph. 4:8; Ps. 68:18). Unlike Saul, the king who takes (8:11–17), David and Jesus are kings who use their thrones to give to their people.

Desperate people, like Saul, often pray, but their prayers are often not answered because they ask for the wrong things with wrong motives.

We are like David's two hundred men who were too exhausted to fight, yet received the spoils won by another (30:21–25). Jesus, like David, has gained back more than we lost when Satan defeated Adam. We don't merely regain the status Adam lost; we are better off than Adam was, being enriched with Jesus's perfect righteousness, which can never be lost (30:20; 2 Cor. 8:9; Phil. 3:9). Though we are unworthy, Jesus calls us his brothers (30:23; Luke 8:21; Heb. 2:11, 17; John 15:13–15).

How does this passage apply to us?

- Desperate people, like Saul, often pray, but their prayers are often not answered because they ask for the wrong things with wrong motives (28:6; James 4:3).

- People today still turn to the occult, seeking guidance. Don't dabble in what God has forbidden or hidden (Deut. 29:29; 18:9–13; Isa. 46:9). Not all spirituality is equally valid. We should seek God's guidance only through his infallible, all-sufficient Word (2 Tim. 3:16–17; 2 Peter 1:3).
- Saul's final days are a picture of what happens to those who turn their backs upon God. Though they may seem to prosper for a while, their end will be terrible.
- In light of Saul's tragic example, seek the Lord while he may be found (Isa. 55:6–7), lest you harden your heart to the point that you, like Saul, are beyond recovery (Heb. 3:8, 15). Don't wait to turn to God, because one day it will be too late (Luke 16:25–26). It is an awful thing to be separated from God (Isa. 13:8; 1 Thes. 5:3).
- Saul's demise also serves as a reminder of our duty to call others to God before it is too late.
- Though David was probably facing the consequences of his unwise choices to hide among the Philistines when Ziklag was raided, he turned to the Lord in his trial and the Lord strengthened and helped him (30:6–8). Sometimes it is good that we face affliction, because our afflictions drive us back to God (Ps. 119:67, 71).
- Though the Lord had determined to give David victory over the Amalekites, David had to rapidly pursue them and fight against them (30:8–20). God uses means, including our efforts and our obedience, to accomplish his good purposes; for example, evangelism, through which God saves the lost, work in our vocations, through

which God provides our daily bread, and the discipline of our children, through which the Lord delivers them from foolishness.

- God's enemies will be like the Amalekites on the day of judgment. They will be totally unprepared, eating and drinking on the day of their doom (30:16; Matt. 24:38–39).
- We, like David, should give glory to God for everything good we accomplish in this life (30:23). "What do you have that you did not receive? And if you did receive it, why do you boast as if you had not received it?" (1 Cor. 4:7). Some, like David's men, who were proud of their accomplishment (30:22), need to be reminded of this.
- Our realization that every good thing we have is from God should humble us and make us, like David, generous with those who don't have as much as we have (30:24–25). We, like David, should honor the weak among us (1 Cor. 12:4–7).

FOR FURTHER STUDY

1. What does the Bible teach about astrology, séances, and fortune-telling? Read Deuteronomy 18:9–14. May a believer be involved in such things, if it is just for fun?
2. Should Christians avoid fiction, such as the Harry Potter books, in which witchcraft is portrayed favorably?
3. Should we be concerned about demonic powers in our day (1 Cor. 10:19–20)? What can we do to oppose them? Read James 4:7 and Ephesians 6:10–20.
4. In what sense would Saul soon join Samuel, given that Samuel was a believer and Saul appears to have been an unbeliever under God's judgment (see 2 Sam. 12:23; Ps. 49:15)?
5. Why did the people of Jabesh-gilead go to so much trouble to give Saul and his sons a proper burial (31:11–13; ch. 11; also see 2 Sam. 21:12–14)?
6. What does the way in which people treat their dead say about their worldview?
7. Why have Christians traditionally favored burial over cremation? Read Ecclesiastes 6:3; Genesis 15:15; 23:4, 19; 25:9–10; 35:8, 29; 49:31; 50:5, 13–14; 2 Kings 9:10, 35–36; Jeremiah 22:19; John 19:39–42; Acts 2:29; 8:2.

TO THINK ABOUT AND DISCUSS

1. What should a believer do if he or she has been involved in occult practices before conversion (Acts 19:19)?
2. Where should we seek guidance from God?
3. How can Christians be guilty of seeking guidance in ways which resemble paganism?
4. Was David wrong to have fled to the Philistines (1 Sam. 27)? Should he simply have trusted God to protect him?
5. Were David's lies to the Philistines justified?
6. Was the capture of the women and children at Ziklag the consequence of David's sin (30:3)?
7. How do the consequences of David's sin compare with the consequences Saul faced for his sin?
8. What consequences do we face when we sin?
9. Where in this final section can we see the gospel?

Endnotes

Chapter 2

1 For more information about dealing with rebellious kids, see Elyse Fitzpatrick and Jim Newheiser, with Dr. Laura Hendrickson, *When Good Kids Make Bad Choices* (Eugene, OR: Harvest House, 2005).

2 For more information about the responsibilities of parents to their adult children, see Jim Newheiser and Elyse Fitzpatrick, *You Never Stop Being a Parent: Thriving in Relationship with Your Adult Children* (Phillipsburg, NJ: P&R, 2010).

Chapter 4

1 C. H. Spurgeon, "Three Decisive Steps," in *Metropolitan Tabernacle Pulpit*, vol. 37, sermon 2220, p. 457; accessed at www.spurgeon.org/sermons/2220.htm.

Chapter 5

1 Michael S. Hamilton, "The Dissatisfaction of Francis Schaeffer: Part 2," in *Christianity Today*, March 3, 1997; accessed at www.christianitytoday.com/ct/1997/march3/7t322b.html.

2 R. C. Sproul, "Statism," at Ligonier Ministries, www.ligonier.org/learn/articles/statism/. Accessed September 2011.

3 Cited under "Power Corrupts; Absolute Power Corrupts Absolutely" at *The Phrase Finder*: www.phrases.org.uk/meanings/. Accessed September 2011.

Chapter 9

1 "VeggieTales: Dave and the Giant Pickle," at: www.imdb.com/. Accessed September 2011.

Additional resources

Commentaries on 1 Samuel

Davis, Dale Ralph, *1 Samuel: Looking on the Heart* (Fearn: Christian Focus, 2000)

Keddie, Gordon J., *Dawn of a Kingdom: The Message of 1 Samuel* (Welwyn: Evangelical Press, 1988)

Audio sermons on 1 Samuel

Visit the Web site of Grace Bible Church, www.grcbible.org, for thirty-three sermons (audio and outlines) preached by the author on 1 Samuel.

Books on topics raised in 1 Samuel

Jones, Robert, *Uprooting Anger: Biblical Help for a Common Problem* (Phillipsburg, NJ: P&R, 2005)

Fitzpatrick, Elyse, and Newheiser, Jim, with Hendrickson, Dr. Laura, *When Good Kids Make Bad Choices* (Eugene, OR: Harvest House, 2005)

Newheiser, Jim, and Fitzpatrick, Elyse, *You Never Stop Being a Parent: Thriving in Relationship with Your Adult Children* (Phillipsburg, NJ: P&R, 2010)